GIVE IT ALL YOU GOT!

UNLEASHING YOUR ENTREPRENEURIAL SPIRIT!

QUINN M. GENTRY, PHD, MBA

Published by:

Messages of Empowerment Productions, LLC: Atlanta, Georgia

ISBN: 978-0-9968167-0-0

MESSAGES OF EMPOWERMENT
Productions, LLC

All rights reserved. No part of this book may be reproduced or transmitted in any form or by any means, electronic or mechanical, including photographing, recording or by any information storage and retrieval system without written permission from the author, except for the inclusion of brief quotations in a review.

Book Cover Designer: Elaine Young, Hopscotch Communications
Project Editors: Eric "Bo" Foston, Gwen Julien, and William C. Jones

Copyright © 2016 by Quinn M. Gentry
First Edition, 2016

Printed and Published in the United States of America

This book is dedicated to my family members who taught me how to blend hard work with honest hustle, my mentors who modeled the way, my clients who trusted my advice, my TEAM-MOE courageous followers, and my soul mate who inspired me to finish strong.

"the entrepreneurial spirit"

"I don't think I can take much more of this," she confided. "Do you trust my advice?" I asked. "I do, "she whispered. "Then before you give up, give in, or give out, let me work with you to take one last shot to give it all you got!" "Can you help me?" she uttered with a cracking voice. "I will," as I asserted in my Dr. Quinn Motivates voice....

"Let's Go!"

TABLE OF CONTENTS

ABOUT THE AUTHOR	*vii*
ABOUT MESSAGES OF EMPOWERMENT, LLC	*ix*
FOREWORD BY DR. ROBERT YANCEY	*x*
ACKNOWLEDGEMENTS.	*xii*
PREFACE	*xiii*
INTRODUCTION	*xvii*

CHAPTER NO.	CHAPTER TITLE	PAGE NO.
1	**ARE YOU READY TO SHIFT FROM A CAREER TO A CALLING?** *It takes drive to move from a career to a calling.*	21
2	**DO YOU HAVE A HEALTHY FLOW OF AUTHENTIC ENTHUSIASM?** *The ultimate source of your enthusiasm must be supernatural.*	41
3	**ARE YOU WILLING TO RE-PURPOSE YOUR PAST?** *Never underestimate the power of your past struggles.*	61
4	**DO YOU HAVE A CLEARLY DEFINED BRAND?** *Before you can sell "it" you must sell "you."*	79
5	**HAVE YOU MASTERED BUSINESS MANAGEMENT 101?** *You must master the backroom operations.*	95
6	**HAVE YOU BUILT A VISION FOR YOUR DREAM TEAM?** *You need a core team of courageous followers.*	117
7	**DO YOU HAVE A GROWTH AND MAINTENANCE PLAN?** *You must grow the top line and maintain the bottom line.*	145
8	**CAN YOU ACCEPT DEFEAT, BUT NOT FAILURE?** *Let failure be the fuel that drives you forward when you feel like giving up.*	159
9	**DO YOU HAVE A PROPER PERSPECTIVE ON YOUR PRIORITIES?** *Value and honor your agreements.*	171
10	**ARE YOU PREPARED TO PUNCH A CLOCK THAT NEVER STOPS?** *Before giving up your "9-5," be very clear that you can execute "24-7."*	183
	Recommendations for 100 books to help keep YOUR "DRIVING" skills sharp	203

About The Author

Quinn M. Gentry, PhD, MBA
quinn.gentry@team-moe.com | www.team-moe.com

President & CEO | Social & Behavioral Scientist | Executive Coach | Author | Speaker
Spoken Word Artist | Playwright

Dr. Quinn M. Gentry (affectionately known as "Dr. Quinn") is President and CEO of Messages of Empowerment Productions, LLC (TEAM-MOE) – a public health and management consulting company located in Atlanta, GA that specializes in organizational effectiveness, women's health, program evaluation, and community engagement. Prior to launching her own business, Dr. Quinn worked as a corporate executive for several Fortune 500 companies, including Johnson & Johnson, Kimberly-Clark, and Wal-Mart corporations. She also served as a Political Intelligence Officer at the Central Intelligence Agency (CIA) and later held behavioral research and teaching positions at Emory University and Georgia State University. Dr. Quinn's more than 25 years of leadership experience in government, corporate, and non-profit organizations contribute to her being highly respected and a sought-after workshop facilitator, consultant, and public speaker.

Her prior leadership and officer positions held include: Technical Leader and Program Director for multiple sponsored research projects; President of the *Black Affairs Program* for the CIA; and she served seven years as Chair of the *Leadership Summit* for the National Coalition of 100 Black Women Inc. - Metropolitan Atlanta Chapter. In addition, Dr. Quinn is a former Program Director for the 100 Black Men's (The Atlanta Chapter) Project Success Mentoring Program and Founder and Managing Director of The Inner-City Achievers Foundation. Other select professional accolades include – past recipient of the Texas Christian University (TCU) Leadership Award, valedictorian of the 2013 Small Business Administration's (SBA) Emerging Leaders Program, recipient of the Red Pump Award for her work in HIV Prevention and Intervention, and the recipient of the Center for Black Women's Wellness 20th Anniversary Health Leader Award.

Dr. Quinn is known primarily for her work as a social and behavioral scientist and subject matter expert (SME) on a wide range of social issues and health threats affecting women and girls. She has also served as a Principal Investigator, Senior Scientist, and Research Analyst on numerous assessment and evaluation studies at the federal, state, and local government levels. As an executive leadership coach, Dr. Quinn has conducted workshops and customized sessions for business and community leaders, managers, frontline, and technical staff, as well as for entrepreneurs and the faith-based community. She has authored over 50 publications and presented at top-tier professional conferences in the fields of public and women's health, HIV/AIDS, and sociology. Dr. Quinn has also authored 11 books on a broad range of topics, namely leadership, entrepreneurship, program evaluation, mentoring, and black feminism.

Dr. Quinn completed a post-doctoral fellowship at the Johns Hopkins University Bloomberg School of Public Health and holds a Ph.D. degree in Sociology from Georgia State University. She earned an M.B.A. degree in Marketing from Clark Atlanta University and completed her undergraduate studies at Texas Christian University where she received a B.A. degree with dual majors in Political Science and History, and a minor in International Relations.

Dr. Quinn is a licensed minister and graduate of the Women's Institute of Ministry, and has served as a course instructor for the Bible Institute at Elizabeth Baptist Church in Atlanta, GA. She is a native of Atlanta where she grew up in the inner-city's Perry Homes Community.

About Messages of Empowerment Productions, LLC

Messages of Empowerment Productions, LLC (TEAM-MOE) is a management consulting firm specializing in public health, new program development, organization effectiveness, and knowledge dissemination. Headquartered in Atlanta, Ga., TEAM-MOE achieves its business objectives through an extensive national network of dedicated subject matter experts and small consulting firms.

Our Mission
TEAM-MOE contributes to the process of changing: **(1)** individual lives, **(2)** organizations, **(3)** communities, **(4)** systems, and **(5)** structures in a way that enhances social and health opportunities for vulnerable populations.

Our Vision
TEAM-MOE accomplishes its mission by: Evaluating Programs * Educating Providers * Empowering People * Engaging the Public

Our Four (4) Practice Areas
TEAM-MOE is organized into four (4) main practice areas: (1) Program Evaluation; (2) Organizational Effectiveness; (3) Social and Behavioral Intervention; and (4) Community Engagement and Knowledge Dissemination.

Subject Matter Expertise
TEAM-MOE's staff and affiliates have expertise in the following subject matter areas: Adolescent Girls Development * Business, Brand Management, and Entrepreneurship * Child Welfare and Juvenile Justice * Faith-based Programs and Interventions * HIV/AIDS/STDs Awareness, Monitoring and Management * Homelessness and Supportive Housing * Leadership Development * Maternal and Child Health * Mentoring and After-school Programs * Organizational Capacity and Effectiveness * Social and Structural Determinants of Health * Substance Abuse and Mental Health Treatment and Aftercare * Teen Pregnancy Prevention and Intervention Treatment Court and Supportive Services * Violence against Women * Women and Girls Health

Foreword by Dr. Robert Yancey

Dr. Quinn Gentry's new book, "Give It All You Got" is a valuable resource for anyone contemplating business ownership. It is especially so for those who were raised in an environment where parents, relatives, nor close friends were business owners...whose upbringing could not include the benefit of a "business tradition." With this book, Dr. Quinn becomes the role model, who provides affirmation, confirmation, and education to potential business owners. As a representative of this demographic, who did create a business, she understands the peculiar issues that inhibit, intimidate, and obstruct many of her peers from pursuing viable business opportunities, and she presents her proven strategy for mitigating, minimizing, and overcoming those issues.

Dr. Quinn was raised in Atlanta's "Perry Homes" community. At that time, it was one of the most challenging urban environments in America. It was a neighborhood where one was as likely to go to jail as to college. With the exception of the faculty and staff of Archer High School, from which she graduated, it was a community bereft of local business ownership or professional role models.

My history with Dr. Quinn began when she returned to Atlanta after having given up a prestigious corporate management position, to join the staff of a member-driven, community development organization, named "100 Black Men of Atlanta," where I am a member. This organization of African American men has committed itself to expanding educational opportunities for children of Atlanta's least privileged communities. For our initial project, "Project Success," we adopted an eighth-grade class at Archer High School, Dr. Quinn's alma mater, and we promised to pay the higher education expenses of everyone in that class who graduated high school. Our members became one-on-one mentors with the students, and remarkably, the entire class graduated, and enrolled in post-secondary educational institutions. As the 100 Black Men expanded Project Success to include more students at more schools, we reached out to Dr. Quinn to join our professional staff and to lend her professional expertise to our mentoring and intervention efforts.

Soon after her return to Atlanta, Dr. Quinn found herself engaged in the practice of entrepreneurship. Her initial venture was more accidental than intentional. Her best friend since childhood requested her assistance in fielding a research study to examine the feasibility of implementing a leadership development program among youth in foster care. Dr. Quinn's participation led to such success that she was awarded a long-term contract with the organization. That was the genesis of what has evolved into a family of business products and services related to empowering people who live in challenged communities. She has analyzed the processes involved in founding and growing her opportunity to a successful business, and she has applied those processes in assisting several of her contemporaries in starting successful businesses. In "Give it All You Got," Dr. Quinn delivers this development process for successful entrepreneurship In 10 content-rich chapters. Her message, "Maybe you can...here's who...here's how!" This is not a "feel good" book that encourages everyone to enter business. Instead, Dr. Quinn outlines the personal attributes of those who could succeed in business, as well as those who should keep their day jobs.

I was, and remain, very impressed with Dr. Quinn's wealth of knowledge and experience, her organizational skills, her drive, her integrity, and the highly successful outcomes that her work achieves. Based upon my background as a student, and practitioner of entrepreneurship, I can affirm that the content of "Give It All You Got" reflects the fundamentals and essentials for starting ones' own business. I am impressed with Dr. Quinn's highly effective style of communicating and conveying her message. And I know that it will be resonant and empowering to the audience toward which it is directed. Moreover, there is wisdom here for everyone.

Robert J. Yancy, Ph.D.
Professor Emeritus
(Founding) Dean, School of Management
Southern Polytechnic State University (Kennesaw State University)
Author: "Federal Government Policy and Black Business Enterprise

ACKNOWLEDGEMENTS

"Give it All You Got" emerged as a result of work done through Messages of Empowerment Productions, LLC (TEAM-MOE). For over a decade, I helped individuals embrace their entrepreneurial spirit. I am forever grateful to them for trusting my advice and connecting with my unique brand of motivation that is part enthusiasm and part experiential.

Many individuals have contributed to the content of this book. As I went from working one-on-one to conducting workshops, I gathered feedback and ideas from every experience that was invaluable in transferring the workshop material into a manuscript. To begin with, this book would not have been possible without the support from my clients and staff at TEAM-MOE. You all trusted the learning laboratory phenomenon where we partnered in testing and refining the advice now documented in this volume. To all those who worked with me in providing insights, critical feedback, and creative suggestions: Thank You!

I am especially grateful to those who called, wrote, or emailed to express how my workshops genuinely inspired and informed your approach to business development and growth. I cannot express how personally inspiring and encouraging your words have been.

Thank you Commissioner Kelly Robinson. As I was putting the final touches on this book, you whispered, "You're just getting started." Thank you for rejuvenating me and encouraging me to unleash my gifts and talents on multiple dimensions.

Thank you to my best friend, Tyronda Minter, for giving me my very first contract as an entrepreneur. I hope I make you proud.

Preface

The inspiration for this book derived from my God-given gifts to motivate, educate, and empower people to live their best lives both professionally and personally. These talents have afforded me opportunities to serve in a variety of capacities and positions which validated for me that I was born to coach and inspire people. My "calling" was pronounced in 2010 during the aftermath of the *"Great Recession,"* when several influential colleagues reached out to me seeking guidance and inspiration as they weathered unprecedented personal, financial, emotional, and relationship challenges stemming from the prolonged impact of the recession.

The Great Recession of 2007-09 officially lasted from December 2007 to June 2009. Historically it is recognized as the largest economic downturn since the Great Depression. The root cause of the Great Recession is connected to the collapse of the eight (8) trillion dollar housing market, which resulted in a domino effect in the consumer spending market. When the dust finally settled, the U.S. labor market lost between 8-10 million jobs. Unemployment and underemployment triggered abnormally high levels of "involuntary part-time" and "marginally attached" workers.

Nothing prepared middle class America for such a devastating economic downturn. Unfortunately, its effect led to increased "out of character" behavior stemming from desperation and depression. Most alarming was the extreme fear, anger, and despair exhibited by men and women who prided themselves on being sound personal financial stewards.

In 2010 I began receiving calls and requests from people seeking counsel on how to manage stressors resulting from the economic crisis. While advising and guiding colleagues and associates on enduring the financial crisis a recurrent theme emerged which I later termed the *"reluctant entrepreneur."* Reluctant entrepreneurs are individuals who previously held stable, highly skilled positions, who are forced to become entrepreneurs by circumstances beyond their control rather than by choice. These individuals were accustomed to middle to upper-middle class lifestyles complete with home ownership, retirement accounts, health insurance, and disposable income for family vacations and luxury goods.

My "enthusiastic pep-talks" were appreciated as my friends and colleagues continued to call upon me, but I sensed that I was no match for the gloomy updates of demotion, downsizing, bankruptcy, defaults on student loans, returning leased luxury vehicles, walking away from upside down home mortgages, and perhaps the most devastating toll of all was the dissolution of, what I deemed as an outside observer to be, solid, stable, and loving marriages and families. I continued to coach and motivate, but over time it proved to be too little, and too late for the size of the financial and emotional suffering I was witnessing. I knew I had to do something different to have a greater impact.

As a matter of fact, over a three-year period I encountered several reluctant entrepreneurs. One particular phone conversation stands out: "Quinn I don't think I can do this much longer. I need to talk to somebody ... I'm just reaching out." I later met with this individual and listened as she recounted her story. She expressed shame and guilt for having to downsize the family home and lifestyle they were accustomed to. And when seeking employment she reported experiencing high levels of anxiety and stress as she took the rejection personally. This individual observed and remarked on my entrepreneurial growth and success over the past few years during the recession. She was inspired and motivated by my enthusiasm and optimism. In an attempt to infuse humor and make light of the situation, I chimed in, "Girl when you have been poor before, hustling to make ends meet is not that difficult." We chuckled as I shared all the (legal) side hustles I had growing up and on into my collegiate and early career years.

As we continued our conversations over the next few months, I realized there was a need for coaching this group of entrepreneurs who stumbled upon business ownership as a necessary survival technique initially, but needed a special blend of motivation and technical-know how to establish and build the business. This motivated me to develop a business coaching model that would transform *"reluctant entrepreneurs"* into *"authentic entrepreneurs."* The transformational process entails personal growth and development, business strategic planning, brand management consulting, and sustained motivation. Using this model, authentic entrepreneurs uncover buried talents, transferrable skills, competencies, confidence, and courage to give entrepreneurship their best shot.

What I realized through this experience, however, is that not everyone is cut out to be an authentic business owner. Some individuals are clearly not suited or equipped to succeed in an entrepreneurial environment or manage the associated inherent risks. Nevertheless, this should in no way be viewed as failure. There is nothing to be ashamed of if a decision is made to revert to employee status. As the old adage states, "Nothing beats a failure but a try!"

In fact, individuals who have explored entrepreneurship are better prepared to reintegrate into the workplace. To be clear, the Great Recession revolutionized every work environment, including corporate, government, and non-profit in ways that leaders and decision-makers now embody more of an entrepreneurial spirit. In this way, my coaching strategy proved "win-win" as several of my clients who ultimately transitioned back into employment, rather than continue to pursue business ownership, returned to the workforce with a greater appreciation for the challenges their innovative and strategic leaders face.

In my closing conversation with clients opting to return to employment status, I encouraged them to take on the role of "courageous followers" as a way to apply core principles of entrepreneurship in their next endeavor. Courageous followers possess the necessary skills and talents to become excellent managers and leaders in an entrepreneurial environment. I also refer to courageous followers as "intrepreneurs" – those capable of excelling at leading product or service roll-outs, managing high-performing work teams, and following procedures and protocols to a level where authentic entrepreneurs can grow new business while sustaining current business.

Whether you are an authentic entrepreneur or courageous follower, I invite you to explore the ideas, information, and inspiration I provide in the form of ten (10) questions serving as chapter titles. As you answer these fundamental questions, you are designing your own roadmap to drive towards your entrepreneurial destiny!

Let's Go!

Dr. Quinn Motivates

INTRODUCTION

As a behavioral scientist specializing in women and girls' health, I founded Messages of Empowerment Productions, LLC (TEAM-MOE) in 2005 to give voice to people at greater risk for social and health threats in communities of color. Equipped with 20 years of work experience, an MBA, and a Ph.D., I launched my own business with the belief that previous work experience, an advanced education, and genuine enthusiasm for entrepreneurship would be sufficient to take me from zero to 100 as a leading public health consulting firm. Indeed my business got off to a fantastic start. In fact, things were going so well in the start-up years that my firm not only survived the economic downturn of the Great Recession, but also grew by leaps and bounds. The firm flourished to the point that I moved out of my home office to an office building in the heart of the prestigious Buckhead business district in Atlanta, GA.

In 2008, just one (1) year after moving into the new office space and being awarded eight (8) consecutive contracts, we experienced the disappointment of receiving notifications for 13 consecutive rejected contract proposals. Unwilling to accept defeat I collected my thoughts and dove deep into business strategy and preservation mode. I contacted every sponsoring agency that rejected our funding proposals and took detailed, copious notes. I quickly learned the dynamics and politics of securing contracts in the public health industry. I also recognized and acknowledged my firm's lack of technical experience and subject matter expertise in public health. Armed with valuable feedback and insight, I focused on providing excellent service to existing clients while thinking critically about the future of the firm. Over a three-year period, my firm rebounded receiving several small (local) and some major (federal) multi-year contracts.

Around the same timeframe I recognized that other entrepreneurs were not faring quite as well in weathering the economic downturn. So, in 2010, I began conducting workshops with business owners and individuals looking to start a business. Several participants of the workshop wound up hiring me as a life coach to help them address personal issues, as well as build the platform for their brand, and business and operations infrastructure for their enterprise. The work in this area was instrumental in my own rebranding as "Dr. Quinn Motivates," where I combine life coaching techniques with traditional brand management and marketing principles to help mold entrepreneurs into CEOs. In this sense, this book has been a journey of sorts for me as I transitioned from motivating and encouraging close associates who were "reluctant entrepreneurs" to life coaching professionals who discovered their passion for business ownership.

The purpose of this book is to provide guiding principles and best practices for entrepreneurs on comprehensive tasks related to starting, growing, and sustaining a profitable business. The chapters provide the insight needed to make it on your entrepreneurial journey. While no single book for entrepreneurs contains all the information needed to launch a successful business, I constructed comprehensive checklists of mandatory tasks for all entrepreneurs. Adapted from my personal experiences as an authentic entrepreneur and loosely based on my hands-on experience conducting workshops on entrepreneurship, this book includes true and candid recounts of the tough decisions and risks that come with the territory of entrepreneurship.

Entrepreneurship is far more than just an idea or creative brainstorm related to a new product or service. It is a complex set of steps aimed at turning creative thoughts into profits. In fact, I was inspired to write a book that bridged the gap between the two extremes of primary writings on entrepreneurship. On one hand, there are technical manuals that provide structure for a business plan. On the other hand, there are motivational books that inspire entrepreneurs to take action. I set out to blend technical tasks and motivational messages. In this way, this book is designed to help entrepreneurs establish and strengthen their brands and to adopt a strong business and operations infrastructure. The technical guidance is fortified with motivational messages to encourage entrepreneurs to go the distance particularly during times of adversity.

Part 1: Conceptualizing the Personal Commitment to Entrepreneurship

The first three (3) chapters are personal and require undertaking intense, transparent analysis to determine if you are ready to commit to an entrepreneurial way of life. At the conclusion of part one (1), entrepreneurs should understand the responsibility for taking full ownership of being in the "drivers" seat.

Part 2: Business Planning, Brand Management, and Team-Building

Chapters four (4) through six (6) highlight detailed activities for business planning and early product or service launch. This phase of entrepreneurship is about developing a roadmap, and customizing business monitoring dashboards to gauge performance as you prepare to go the distance. During this phase you also make preliminary decisions about the types of passengers that will ride in the car as 'dream team" members.

Part 3: Growing, Sustaining, and Failing Better

Chapters seven (7) and eight (8) provide strategies for

advancing into the "fast lane" and developing coping strategies for "crashes" on any given day on the entrepreneurial highway. Over time, you learn to maintain multiple lanes as you manage existing business and gear up to take advantage of growth opportunities.

Part 4: Synchronizing Priorities and the Pursuit of Entrepreneurship

The final phase, chapters nine (9) and ten (10), entails using the "cruise control" feature as you master the process of balancing business management and personal life priorities. At this point in the entrepreneurial journey, you should focus on institutionalizing the principles and best practices that serve as the foundation for the entrepreneurial lifestyle.

DRIVING LESSONS LEARNED. At the conclusion of each chapter I highlight my own battle-tested responses to each of the questions I now pose to other entrepreneurs. I made lots of mistakes and missteps but never failed in the traditional definition of failure. I learned how to work more effectively and learned to embrace "failure" as opportunities for growth. Some of my best learned lessons in business were painful, some were quite expensive. However, I vowed to turn those mistakes into examples of what "not to do." Over time these experiences grew into wisdom; and wisdom became the seeds of success for coaching others on pursuing entrepreneurial endeavors.

To gain the full benefits of my approach you must value patience, perseverance, and the core principles of project management. Without these virtues my executive coaching method will not be effective for you. In my portfolio I promote proven tools and processes, not "get rich quick schemes". I believe in intense planning periods to establish strong foundations. I also promote compliance with government and other regulatory agencies, and establishing personal priorities. If you share my values, principles, and priorities, then this book promises to serve as a blueprint to help you develop your own personal roadmap in preparation for your authentic entrepreneurial "drive."

Authentic Entrepreneurs....
            ...Start your engines....
                        ...Now Let's Go!

CHAPTER 1

ARE YOU READY TO SHIFT FROM A CAREER TO A CALLING?

It takes "DRIVE" to move from a career to a calling!

"I was told by an acquaintance that my relentless drive can be "intimidating"...My response: "Well get ready to be "terrified" as I shift into overdrive!"

Dr. Quinn Motivates

It matters not what product or service provides the platform for your calling to entrepreneurship, the bottom line is you must show up in the entrepreneur world with a kind of "DRIVE" that is unprecedented. Before that "drive" can take shape in the physical, it must begin as a shift in mindset. You have to think, sleep, and embrace every aspect of the entrepreneurial life. I call it "authentic entrepreneurship" where your life and business venture become a real and non-negotiable part of who you are.

There is a cute but true quote circling in social media that defines an entrepreneur as "someone who jumps off a cliff and builds a plane on the way down". This may sound crazy at first glance, but an authentic entrepreneur fully understands all that is packed into this simple analogy. Once you know within your heart of hearts that you are called to pursue entrepreneurship, you have to take that leap of faith and get out of whatever comfort zone you are in and resolve to build the missing pieces along the journey.

In my work as a business strategist, I speak to countless individuals who claim to have heard an inner voice calling them to entrepreneurship. However, once I start to have in-depth discussions about the process and the commitment, as well as the potential toll on one's family and intimate life, many conclude that they simply aren't ready yet. In this first chapter I address the five (5) recurring themes that must be addressed in moving from a "career to a calling." I call it the "DRIVE" model where "DRIVE" is an acronym comprised of five (5) key areas that puts the entrepreneur in the "driver's seat" in preparation for the entrepreneurial journey. Simply put, without "DRIVE", you cannot effectively make the shift from a career to a calling. Definitively, without "DRIVE" you need to stay with your good cooperate or government job with benefits and pray for a respectable retirement plan.

THE "DRIVE" MODEL AT A GLANCE				
D	**R**	**I**	**V**	**E**
DECIDE TO TAKE ACTION	RESOLVE TO UNBLOCK YOUR DRIVE WAY	IGNITE WITH INNOVATION	VALUE YOUR GIFTS AND TALENTS	EXECUTE WITH EXCELLENCE

D: DECIDE TO TAKE ACTION

Deciding to take action is conceptualized as a process comprised of five (5) non-negotiable decisions that must be made. Ralph Waldo Emerson is credited as having said "Once you make a decision, the universe conspires to make it happen." This is exactly what happens for authentic entrepreneurs when they decide to give entrepreneurship everything they have.

Having studied the biographical profiles of hundreds of entrepreneurs it amazes me how many of them were C-average students in high school and/or college, with many actually being college drop-outs and some returning to complete college later in life as a symbolic gesture of goal completion after having been successful as entrepreneurs. As a tribute to all the successful entrepreneurs who were C-students, I have outlined five (5) concrete decisions related to shifting from a career to a calling using "Cs."

DECISION #1: CONFRONT YOUR COMFORT ZONES. Creatures of comfort do not fare well at entrepreneurship. At some point, you must muster up the courage to leave the comforts of a career to follow the uncertainties and uncharted territories along the entrepreneurial journey. As you think about what it will mean to move out of your comfort zone, here are ten (10) paradigm shifts that separate the "employee" from the "entrepreneur".

THE PARADIGM SHIFT FROM THE "CAREER-MIND" TO THE "ENTREPRENEURIAL LIFESTYLE"	
EMPLOYMENT	ENTREPRENEURSHIP
1. Salary 2. Position-driven 3. Promotion 4. Benefits and bonuses 5. The strategic plan 6. Moving up in management 7. Retirement 8. 9 to 5/ 40 hr. work week 9. Work-life balance 10. Co-workers	1. Sales 2. Purpose-driven 3. Passion 4. Growth and maintenance 5. Sustainability 6. Moving out in mission 7. Exit strategy or life-long commitment 8. 24/7 9. Professional and personal prioritizing 10. Collaborators

DECISION #2: HAVE CONFIDENCE IN YOUR COMPETENCIES. I have yet to encounter a successful entrepreneur that felt like they were fully prepared to leave their job and pursue entrepreneurship. Instead, what they all have in common is a commitment and confidence to simply work with what they believed to be God-given competencies and take a leap of faith. Each discovered over time that they had more than enough to live a purpose-driven life. To jumpstart the discovery process, and increase your confidence in your competencies, search your strengths and areas you have excelled at in the natural over the course of your life. Identify those competencies that you strengthened through repetition and continued formal education. Put in writing all the things you do well, and enjoy doing, then think of multiple ways to profit from your competences.

DECISION #3: CALCULATE THE COST. Calculating the cost of entrepreneurship is a three-fold process. First, you must know the costs associated with starting the business. This means you must have a business and marketing plan developed in the early stages. Second, you need to calculate the costs associated with your personal lifestyle and household budget. So many times I have had to do the hard coaching of pointing out that far too many entrepreneurs want to maintain their current lifestyle and that may not be possible in the start-up years. Others complain about not having start-up or expansion capital and it's because they have shopped away assets that could have financed the business at key phases. Simply put, you must learn to live beneath your means. This also means putting family and friends on notice that your disposable income, and interest free loans and gifts will be eliminated for some period of time. The final more sensitive area is entrepreneurship will cost you in time and relationships. Once you calculate the tangible and intangible costs you must make a "go," or "no go" decision.

DECISION #4: HAVE THE COURAGE TO APPEAR CRAZY. Moving from a career to a calling requires the courage to appear crazy on any given day! I am a firm believer that it's a fine line between "courageous" and "crazy" when it comes to authentic entrepreneurship, and only a few of us have the courage to walk it. Cowards cannot be authentic entrepreneurs because of the illogical risks involved. Many people have great business ideas, but when it comes time to "DRIVE", they reject the steps and stages that can't be explained. Having read the backgrounds of many entrepreneurs we all have come to admire, I am convinced that the reason most do not fear looking crazy is because they learned to function in very chaotic environments early in life. Now later in life, what looks like crazy to those from more stable upbringings is just a day in the life for entrepreneurs who gained strength and resilience in surviving dysfunctional homes and scarce resources.

DECISION #5: CLOSE THE DOOR ON ALL OTHER CAREER OPTIONS. At some point you must make a decision to close the door on all other career options and pursue entrepreneurship. I call this decision a "date with destiny," where it is important to literally put a date on the calendar where you intend to be "all in" towards achieving your entrepreneurial goal. When you don't make this definitive date, you enter what I call "the most dangerous phase in the life of an authentic entrepreneur," where you are working at a job and doing just enough to keep from getting fired and they are paying you just enough to keep you from quitting. Be sure when you leave your career for a calling that you are not running from something that is unpleasant in your current work environment, because I guarantee you that whatever that monster is, it will show up in your entrepreneurial pursuit. To avoid the pitfalls of this danger zone, you must set a decision day to officially leave the corporate world and under what conditions. The decision to leave should not be motivated by an emotional uptick when you are having a bad day at the office. Instead, it should be a methodical, strategic, and intentional decision to pursue entrepreneurship. Other doors that you will be closing as you make the transition to entrepreneurship include leaving behind "the taken-for-granted" business and operations departments that support your current position, such as human resources, technology, legal, sales and marketing, finance and accounting, as well as daily contact and socializing with work friends and associates in the work environment.

R: RESOLVE TO "UNBLOCK" YOUR DRIVEWAY

No matter how passionate you are about the pursuit of entrepreneurship after deciding to take action, the next step is to unblock your driveway. Unblocking the driveway entails removing those roadblocks that are barriers to your pursuit. Here are some common roadblocks that that can hinder your drive: (1) inner-me blocks; (2) financial blocks; (3) intimate partner blocks; and (4) family and friends blocks.

REMOVING THINGS THAT ARE BLOCKING YOUR DRIVEWAY

ROADBLOCK 1: INNER-ME BLOCKS. The "inner-me" blocks are those self-sabotaging thoughts and actions that deter your entrepreneurial pursuit. The good news is that this entire book is dedicated to addressing the "inner-me." Don't confuse the "enemy" with the "inner-me" as this makes it convenient to shift blame and responsibility to someone else for the lack of progress towards achieving your entrepreneurial goals. Common "inner-me" blocks include: (1) limited to no self-efficacy; (2) fear of being labeled incompetent; (3) negative self-talk surfacing from old messages from childhood; (4) the need for certainty and security; and (5) fear of failure. As a starting point for removing the blocks associated with the "inner-me," use the following activities to de-clutter your mind, thereby paving the way for clarity towards your entrepreneurial calling. The activities include:

1. Develop a finite and simple purpose-driven statement that reflects your overall entrepreneurial pursuit.
2. Document three (3) resources you need to accomplish your entrepreneurial purpose.
3. Detail the strategies that you will pursue to accomplish your entrepreneurial purpose.
4. Delineate the daily priorities that reflect the tasks that must be completed to fulfill your entrepreneurial purpose.

ROADBLOCK 2: FINANCIAL BLOCKS. Entrepreneurship requires proper financial planning. If your entrepreneurial pursuit is predicated upon someone else bearing the brunt of the bills, more than likely, you are setting yourself up for some problems as you may encounter issues with the person maintaining the household bills and lifestyle. The best way to address financial blocks is to condition yourself to live "BENEATH" your means. For me, I applied Suze Orman's principles of personal finance. Following her general advice resulted in my returning a leased Mercedes, and instead driving a 15 year-old Honda Accord until the bottom literally fell out; then purchasing in cash a three (3) year-old Volkswagen Beatle that I drove for the first five (5) years of running my business. By my 40th birthday I put a down payment of $20,000.00 in cash on a BMW, and assumed a 3-year loan at a three (3) percent interest rate from a credit union to finance the balance. I was selected as a National Institute of Health Clinical Researcher where the program paid $40,000.00 of my $78,000.00 accumulative student loans for my bachelors, masters, and PhD degrees. I devised a plan to pay the balance of $38,000.00 in three (3) years. In terms of lifestyle changes, I reduced my clothes shopping budget, sacrificed hair and nail appointments, and limited vacations from three (3) per year to one (1) per year. To avoid conflict with the person I was married to during the start-up years, I established a household expense account where I put 24-months of my half of the household bills, mortgage, insurance, taxes, and utilities in a money market account so that he would never experience paying any bills on my behalf. Even that was not enough to make him happy with my progress and success as an entrepreneur, but that candid conversation is for another time. The point here is I did everything possible to remove financial roadblocks.

ROADBLOCK 3: INTIMATE PARTNER BLOCKS. One of the most devastating roadblocks of all is to discover that an intimate partner does not support your entrepreneurial pursuit. In fact, as I interact with highly successful women entrepreneurs in particular, there is a repeated theme that their intimate partner relationship suffered as they became more successful. This is a very sensitive issue and one I faced personally. I will say that your decision to work through this particular roadblock is very emotional and complicated. As a starting point, it is important to recognize that all the issues that were already wrong or dysfunctional in your relationship will become even more difficult to deal with, as you set out to pursue entrepreneurship. Some partners are vulnerable enough to express their fears and concerns; while others are passive-aggressive and will behave in ways to message their disapproval of your endeavors. A small percentage will outright sabotage your efforts. Unfortunately for some of my clients, a few partners became aggressive to the point of violence. In addressing this roadblock many discover that the relationship has other unresolved issues as well. Some get through it and emerge as a stronger couple. Others attempt to work around the non-supportive partner. A few decide to walk away as the best option for removing this delicate roadblock. My advice is to do the work to save the relationship to the extent possible with the understanding that it takes two committed individuals to remove this roadblock for the good.

ROADBLOCK 4: FAMILY & FRIENDS BLOCKS. For the most part, family and friends typically are enthusiastic and even inspired by your entrepreneurial dreams. Perhaps the biggest challenge with this group is that you will be emotionally, socially, and financially unavailable to those who rely upon your support in these key areas. Chapter nine (9) on priorities can help you with this group. Because of the close and historical ties you may have to family and friends, when they don't support you, it is likely that you will spend a lot of wasted energy trying to win this group over. Some of their concerns may be legitimate because on some level they do know you and perhaps do have your best interest at heart. In this case, if you can listen to their criticism and concerns as constructive feedback, family and friend blocks could be re-purposed as well-needed sounding boards. However, be mindful that some family and friends who have come to depend on you for various things in their own lives might fear your decisions as a direct threat to their livelihood. To address this block, commit to address your issues of survivor's guilt, or the need for approval and praise.

I: IGNITE WITH INNOVATION

In all of my corporate executive positions I have always worked in new business development where creating something new from concept to market was just a pure passion of mine. In this capacity I had the opportunity to participate in a number of innovative activities that sparked my creativity. As an entrepreneur you must do more than merely carry recording devices, pads, and pens to document bright ideas. You must add to those tools some "outside-the-box" activities to keep your innovative edge to facilitate new ideas and concepts.

STRATEGIES FOR IGNITING INNOVATIION

INNOVATIVE IGNITER 1: CREATE ANNUAL VISION BOARDS. Commit to developing at least one (1) vision board every year. I have been known to create two (2) or three (3) boards within the same calendar year as I am inspired. Use pictures, words, and motivational quotes, and then place your vision board where you can see it on a daily basis if possible. Spend time interacting with it and reviewing what the various images represent. Be sure your vision board incorporates the following components:

CORE COMPONENTS OF A COMPREHENSIVE VISION BOARD

V   **VISUALIZE VICTORY:** What's the end game?

I   **INSPIRATIONAL IMAGES:** What does a successful you look like?

S   **STRATEGIES FOR SUCCESS:** How do you visually capture yourself in action achieving victory?

I   **INNOVATIVE IDEAS:** What symbols and images reflect those parts of your entrepreneurial pursuit that blur the lines of creative and crazy?

O   **OWN YOUR DREAMS:** What reminds you to push past odds and obstacles?

N   **NO LIMITS FOR THINKING BEYOND YOUR "NOW":** What demonstrates your willingness to think big about your future?

INNOVATIVE IGNITER 2: STRIKE UP CONVERSATIONS WITH PEOPLE OTHERS CALL CRAZY OR WEIRD. I call these "no nothing" conversations. If your business centers on interaction with people, then you should make it a common practice to engage people on a regular basis that at first glance have nothing in common with your business. Talk about life in general. Share as much about you as they share about themselves. Resist the need to conform to traditional rules of networking. Simply talk and go with the flow.

INNOVATIVE IGNITER 3: REVERT TO A STATE OF CHILDHOOD. One of the best ways to jumpstart your creative energy is to genuinely play with little kids between the ages of three (3) and ten (10) on their level. Some suggested activities include watch cartoons, wear colorful pajamas, eat cereal, allow them to select the groceries, or color in coloring books. Visit the kiddie sections of a library or bookstore. Take some "little people" to the zoo, amusement park, or a child-centered museum, and allow them to set the agenda for the day. To the extent possible resist the need to enforce rules and be an authority figure. Treat these little ones like consultants and ask lots of questions that require more than a "yes or no" response. If done effectively you should leave this process rejuvenated, detoxed of adult learning theory and practices, and open to options and possibilities that once seemed impossible or impractical.

INNOVATIVE IGNITER 4: PLAN SOLO EXECUTIVE SESSIONS. Make this a retreat of one if at all possible where you allow your mind to wander, dream, create, and play with ideas that do not have to be filtered, explained logically, and be practical during the innovative phase. Pour out your heart's desires by talking to yourself and communicating with the Divine. Speak your dreams and goals into the universe with a spirit of expectancy. Leave all forms of technology off for long stretches of time and let your body be governed by nature. Eat fresh fruits and drink plenty of water. Read motivational books. Journal and doodle your feelings. Release your thoughts through writing, crying, talking, and praying out loud. Take long walks. Let go of people, places, and things that have been hindering your capacity to renew. Replace toxicity with new thoughts, and fresh ideas.

INNOVATIVE IGNITER 5: BRAINSTORM WITH OTHER CREATIVE MINDS THAT ARE NOT NECESSARILY IN THE SAME LINE OF WORK AS YOU. After spending some time wrapping your brain around your own passions and dreams, engage individuals with creative minds. They don't need to be entrepreneurs per se', but they do need to be creative geniuses. Step outside your comfort zone and diversify your creative brainstorm circle to include people from different races and ethnic backgrounds, socio-economic classes, gender and sexual orientation, age, and industries of expertise.

INNOVATIVE IGNITER 6: COMMIT TO CONSISTENT MARKET RESEARCH. There is no substitute for traditional marketing research. By rigorous marketing research I am referring to proven scientific methods for gathering empirical knowledge, including surveys, in-depth interviews, focus groups, and direct observations. You must remain aligned closely with your client and customer base. Engage directly to people who use your products and services on a regular basis. At a minimum you want to research their demographics, lifestyle, passions, people they interact with, their professional lives, and problems they want to solve in their lives. Also, research industry trends and forecasts, then use that accumulated information to explore innovative ideas for new products and services.

INNOVATIVE IGNITER 7: BE CONTEXT RICH. You need to stay current on the latest, as well as, classic information relative to your industry. Attend workshops. Register for formal classes. Sign up for newsletters. Read trade magazines, as well as attend trade shows. Read blogs and articles by subject matter experts. Join professional associations. Engage in professional communities in social media.

INNOVATIVE IGNITER 8: STAY CURIOUS. Authentic entrepreneurs are constantly asking "why," "why not," and "what-if." In like manner, you must remain curious about how things work, and what is not working well. Explore other environments for the ways in which they solve problems. Respectfully and tactfully find ways to question authority and status quo thinking. Look at things from the awkward angle or the other extreme. I call my quest for curiosity "putting a Dr. Quinn spin on it", where I ask questions and engage in quirky and even murky conversations.

INNOVATIVE IGNITER 9: CREATE A CULTURE THAT REWARDS INNOVATION IN YOUR ENVIRONMENT. You have to find a way to engage people that work for you and with you in the innovation process. Some suggestions include: (1) scheduling quarterly brainstorm meetings; and (2) rewarding innovation. For example, if you need to name a company newsletter, implement a contest where you solicit input and provide a small prize to the winner. Encourage everyone to enter as many times as they can come up with ideas.

Invite creative individuals to join your team for innovative sessions. Play with your team. Engage them in activities that have nothing to do with the work that you do, and watch their creativity come alive over time.

INNOVATIVE IGNITER 10: DRESS UP AS YOUR ALTER EGO AND ACT IT OUT. The purpose of acting out your alter egos is to spark creativity. I pretend to be a choreographer, Broadway play director, talk show host, choir director, and jazz dancer or musician. I have also been known to take on the persona of a sports coach imagining that I am charged with leading a basketball or football team to a championship win. All these personas feed my creativity. These work for me, but you have to find those that work for you.

V - VALUE YOUR GIFTS AND TALENTS

In preparing for the entrepreneurial pursuit, you must place a realistic value on your gifts and talents. If you don't put an appropriate value on your gifts and talents, your entrepreneurial drive will be a symbolic short distance. You will not stay in business for the long haul. Also recognize that gifts come naturally, such as a natural gift of a singing voice, ability to draw, or write. These gifts can be perfected through skills-building. However, expert status comes with experience over time. As you shift in particular from being skills-based to expert-centered, your value increases. As your value increases, you must constantly renegotiate your value proposition in the marketplace to be sure you eventually get paid what you are worth.

STRATEGIES FOR ENHANCING YOUR VALUE PROPOSITION

VALUE ENHANCEMENT 1: CONFIDENCE. Increase your confidence in your gifts and talents. Stop coveting over people's gifts. Stop thinking you need just one more resource or credential before you are ready to take action. Have confidence that your gifts will make room for you in the marketplace.

VALUE ENHANCEMENT 2: WORTH. You must know your worth. First you must believe you have self-worth. If you are a consultant you must know the worth of your expertise in actual monetary terms. In establishing monetary value for your talents, you need to determine a price for your consulting services. I set hourly, daily, and project rates for my diverse areas of expertise. For example, I have prices for consulting opportunities for my expertise in the following positions: behavioral scientist, new program developer, business strategist, health educator, evaluator, technical monitor, key note speaker, and workshop facilitator, just to name a few of the roles I play as a consultant. These collective components of worth are critical in the early years to avoid being demoralized as you remember times when you made much more money from a steady paycheck. Another activity to help with worth is to maintain a list of words describing your self-worth, thereby contributing positively to your self-esteem. I refer to my list as my "I AM list", where I document all the adjectives describing who I am and what I am capable of doing.

VALUE ENHANCEMENT 3: CREDENTIALS. As you are moving and advancing in the market place, there is nothing wrong with committing to sharpening your skills along the way. You want to stay cutting edge sharp and keep a competitive advantage. Enhancing your credentials can be achieved via certifications, licensings, leadership programs, and obtaining formal degrees. The point is to sharpen your skills as you drive through tough terrain and territory. Another option is to hire and partner with people that complement your credentials. For example, if you are a creative type, you want to keep a strong project manager on your team. As you immerse in innovation, a credible project manager will assure that the production process, including critical paths and appropriate use of resources, remains on track.

VALUE ENHANCEMENT 4: CREDIBILITY. Document your credibility as you are affirmed by actual clients and customers in the marketplace. This will help you in developing formal proposals. In addition, request testimonials from satisifed clients and customers. Ask for specific feedback on what they believe you did extremely well in servicing them. Sharing testimonials is especially important in an era where unsatifisied customers can take to social media and leave an electronic paper trail of their dissatifaction. You want to balance that by creating opportunities to share success stories of people utilizing your goods and services.

VALUE ENHANCEMENT 5: EXPERIENCE. Documenting past and present experience is extremely important if you are in the consulting business. You will be surprised at how much your skill set, knowledge, and services are enhanced in a very short period of time based on various consulting projects. Many entrepreneurs neglect to update their resume's with experience gained while providing technical and administrative expertise on business projects for their own company. In addition, you want to highlight those areas where you provided strategic advisement beyond the scope of your contract.

VALUE ENHANCEMENT 6: CAPABILITY. Practice writing strong project and service capability statements. Just as your personal resume' highlights your unique set of experiences and expertise, your capability statement can be conceptualized as your company's resume'. Strategically, writing strong capability statements is a way of combining the best of all the resume's among the people who work for you or with whom you team on projects.

E - EXECUTE WITH EXCELLENCE

No matter your inspiring back story of starting a business against the odds, when customers or clients purchase your product they will all require the same level of efforts and results when it comes to servicing them with excellence. In simple terms, executing with excellence means doing everything necessary to deliver on your brand's promise. Moreover, you need to instill in staff and partners alike that they must adhere to high quality, on-time delivery of goods and services.

"10 DIMENSIONS FOR DRIVING EXELLENCE INTO YOUR MODEL"

In his book, *Why "A" Students work for "C" Students (subtitled "and B students work for the government")*, Robert T. Kiyasaki highlighted the factors that separate captains of industries (the "C" students) from the highly skilled technocrats (the "A" students). As a former college instructor and employer of collegiate students transitioning into the workforce, I tend to agree with Kiyasaki's perspective. In my observations, the fine lines of separation is the "C" student's ability and willingness to drive for excellence with available resources. They think on their feet and make things happen, whereas "A" students use the time to articulate thoroughly why the current circumstances prohibit a decision to execute. As a tribute to "C" students who have an entrepreneurial spirit, I have outlined what it means to drive excellence into your entrepreneurial model using words that begin with the letter "C."

DIMENSION OF EXCELLENCE 1: COMPETENCE. You must commit to sharpening your skills and expertise. There is no substitute for continued learning whether it be formal classroom or informal readings to keep current in your field and ahead of technological breakthroughs. Because it is impossible to know everything about your industry, you should also surround yourself with individuals on staff or as consultants who are experts in the areas in which you are less competent.

DIMENSION OF EXCELLENCE 2: CLASS. Think of class as the way you package and polish your competence. Class is especially important if you are the spokesperson for the firm or brand. Remember, you are seen and summed up before you are heard. Class includes making conscientious choices about speech, wardrobe, image, interaction, disposition, and mannerism.

DIMENSION OF EXCELLENCE 3: CONFIDENCE. Confidence is the outward expression of your self-esteem. For the entrepreneur, confidence must be at the forefront of any brand presentation. Confidence is demonstrated in how you show up in person, interact, and work a room. Confidence is about convincing yourself and other important stakeholders that you can deliver the goods or services you aim to sell. Confidence includes having stage presence. Therefore, if you fear the spotlight, you will need to partner with someone who can pitch the business with confidence.

DIMENSION OF EXCELLENCE 4: CREDIBILITY. As you present yourself and market your product or services, you must appear credible. When you think of the term "credible," attributes like trustworthiness, believabiity, and persuasiveness should come to mind. When you leave a sales opportunity, always review the extent to which you came across as credible. In this day of social media, you can instantly determine if a business is credible through a simple search. When people say their business is spread by word of mouth, they are referring to how people share their positive experiences with the product or service with other potentiial customers. Never lose sight that bad news about your brand can also travel just as quickly as positive credible stories. Credibility is built over time by doing what you say you will do as a business owner.

DIMENSION OF EXCELLENCE 5: CAPACITY. As you scale up and out, be sure you have the capacity to maintain and grow your business in ways that are sustainable. This is why building a team of courageous followers who can maintain the high standards you set is paramount. If you encounter capacity issues, it is important to communicate with the client or simply turn business down to avoid risking your reputation for doing great work in trying to do more work than your time and talent permits.

DIMENSION OF EXCELLENCE 6: CREATIVITY. You have to be courageous enough to step outside the box and the normal flow of business to keep a creative edge. Think of how basketball players participate in modern dance classes to make them more graceful in their footwork and more smooth with their hands to avoid committing fouls. In like manner, find industries or environments that have little to do with your goods or services, but offer you transferable skills by jumpstarting your creativity.

DIMENSION OF EXCELLENCE 7: COOPERATIVE. No matter how competent you are, if you are difficult to work with, you will have limitations in the marketplace. My best friend, Tyronda, calls the intersection of competency and cooperation as the "likeability factor." Don't confuse the likeability factor with being a people pleaser or trying to be popular. The likeability factor, as Tyronda has come to define it, is more like bringing an emotionally intelligent disposition to every business exchange.

DIMENSION OF EXCELLENCE 8. COMPATIBILITY. In building a team, be sure you assess for "fit." Assessing for a compatible fit is a combination of technical know-how, teamwork, capacity to grow, psychological and emotional stability, and trust factors. Trust factors include asking yourself, "Can I trust this person with my clients, my staff, my business, and in essence, my financial future?" As you assess for fit, remember the first group of direct hires will be working very close to you and are likely to be in your personal space. This is especially true if you start the business in your home.

DIMENSION OF EXCELLENCE 9. CONTINUED LEARNING COMMUNITY. Not only must you commit to remaining competent in your chosen field, but you must create a culture of continued learning among those that you add to your team. This can be self-directed and informal to keep abreast in the field or via traditional classroom courses in pursuit of degrees or certifications. You can also hold internal workshops and discussions that ignite excellence in thinking and problem-solving. It can also be as simple as selecting a soft skill or technical topic and facilitating a discussion about it as part of staff meetings.

DIMENSION OF EXCELLENCE 10. CLIENT/CUSTOMER ENGAGEMENT. No matter what, you must invest in spending quality time engaging your clients and customers. This is not to sell them anything, but rather constitutes a genuine interest in getting to know those who value your product or services. Be genuine and unpredictable in connecting in ways that catch them by surprise, but is truly sincere. Social media has made this a bit easier, however it is not a substitute for more professional and intimate engagement.

MY "DRIVING" LESSONS LEARNED
IN SHIFTING FROM A CAREER TO A CALLING

1. **CONFIRMATION.** I accepted that if God gave me the gifts and talents, then God would make it possible for me to pursue my purpose with passion, as well as make provision along the path to finish that which He started in me.

2. **CONFIDENCE.** During dark moments, downturns, and down time, I drew energy from reminiscing about my earlier successful efforts in diverse endeavors as a constant reminder that I am a winner.

3. **CONCEAL THE CALLING.** I learned to be discrete when sharing the details of my calling. Some people took up too much energy in needing a well-documented plan of action. Others were downright envious.

4. **COOL UNDER FIRE.** I was living in an environment with a risk-averse individual who kept me anxious and on edge. I learned to stay focused on the hunt and hustle, and resisted the need to respond to negativity in any shape, form, or fashion.

5. **CARE-FRONTATION.** I spent valuable time sharing my dream and business plan with my ex-spouse. In the end, I had to make a conscience choice to move forward without his full support.

6. **CUT EXPENSES.** I saved 24-months of household expenses by cutting out all luxuries, including spa vacations, luxury cars, cleaning service, and a chef.

7. **CAPITAL GENERATION.** In the early years I took on short-term assignments well-beneath my billable rate to generate growth and operating capital.

8. **CONTINUED LEARNING.** I committed to studying women and girls health issues, as well as pursued a post-doctoral fellowship at The Johns Hopkins University Bloomberg School of Public Health to enhance my subject matter expertise.

9. **COURAGE.** I had to muster up the courage to walk away from everything that no longer contributed to fulfilling the calling on my life.

10. **COMFORTABLE ALONE.** I learned to be comfortable and content in my alone time.

"Once you commit to the entrepreneurial calling, excellence must be a driving force."

Dr. Quinn Motivates

Now let's Go!

CHAPTER 2
DO YOU HAVE A HEALTHY FLOW OF AUTHENTIC ENTHUSIASM?
The ultimate source of your enthusiasm must be supernatural.

> *"Everyone will not understand the journey of an authentic entrepreneur. Stop explaining and justifying the entrepreneurial journey to people who are afraid to leave their jobs. You need that energy as fuel for the "DRIVE."*
>
> Dr. Quinn Motivates

Once you start to apply the "DRIVE" model to jumpstart your entrepreneurial pursuit, somewhere along the journey you will hit speed bumps known as barriers, boundaries, or barricades. The good news is most authentic entrepreneurs are equipped with a relentless spirit to overcome these speed bumps for a continued drive towards your entrepreneurial destiny. However, every now and then, speed bumps are big enough to shake your front end, and send you into a bout of depression and despair. As the person in the driver's seat it is your responsibility to realign and keep it moving. This requires having a healthy flow of "authentic enthusiasm."

Defining authentic enthusiasm. In searching for a very simple definition of authentic enthusiasm I couldn't help but recall growing up in the house with my grandmother who was deeply rooted in the Church of God In Christ. Grandmamma hummed a little song on a daily basis that included a line of "This joy that I have the world didn't give it to me...the world didn't give it and the world can't take it away." I came to realize that no matter how deep and intellectual we try to make it, authentic enthusiasm is just that simple. It is about having a joy that the world didn't give to you, and since the world didn't create it, then the world can't destroy it.

Authentic enthusiasm is that internal courage to push past obstacles and challenges in pursuit of a purpose-driven life. When you are fully committed to pursue entrepreneurship, even the most mundane tasks are completed with unspeakable enthusiasm. This is because you understand that each small task is contributing to the larger purpose. No matter how joyous you are, always be on guard for the "killjoys" who will see you flowing and rather than draw strength from your energy, killjoys will try to dampen your mood. In order to maintain your enthusiasm especially in the creative and innovative phases, avoid being baited into logical conversations. When approached with questions and inquiries that may require some level of logic, simply respond, "I can't explain it. I am just flowing with it right now." Further share that at the appropriate time when all the pieces fall into place you will be happy to provide the full picture of what you have been creating.

As an authentic entrepreneur you cannot afford to allow mixed or negative messages to enter into your innovative space. If you want the vehicle (you) to be the ultimate driving machine, you must take full responsibility for the type of "FUEL" used to power your engine. Here is my four-point formula for "FUEL".

"FUEL"

DR. QUINN'S "FUEL" FORMULA AT A GLANCE			
F	**U**	**E**	**L**
FAITH-BASED MESSAGES	UNIQUE TO MY SITUATION	ENTREPRENUERS' TESTIMONEIS	LISTENING PLEASURE

Faith-based messages. While selling Mary Kay Cosmetics, I was introduced to the concept of God-first, family second, and career, third. This lined up with my faith-based upbringing and reinforced my prayer and meditation time. I started to focus on biblical truths and principles that helped me to accept whatever circumstances came my way. I learned to see God's love through the good things that happened to me, as well as during the dark days where my future was less certain. Every day I read some passage of scripture to strengthen my relationship with God. In addition, reading scripture daily brings discipline and discernment to the entrepreneurial process. Of all the biblical study guides I used over the course of building my business, the four (4) I recommend include: (1) The

King James Version of the Bible; (2) The Prayer of Jabez; (3) The Purpose-driven Life; and (4) The Master Life Series.

In fact, my dedication to integrating these faith-based tools into my daily routine resulted in my writing another book called *"In Pursuit of Purpose: Biblical Guidance for the Entrepreneurial Journey"*, where I identified 52 scripture passages and applied them to the life experiences of a Christian entrepreneur. I would be honored if you would consider my faith-based publication as a biblical study guide in your own quest to integrate relevant faith-based messages into your daily routine as an entrepreneur.

Unique to my current situation. Finding resources and inspiration from people that you share something in common with is a great way to remain enthusiastic. For example, I am constantly looking for examples of successful people who grew up in low-income, dysfunctional households where the adult caregivers were a bit irresponsible. It inspires me to see this unique group's extraordinary drive to achieve against the odds. In addition, I absolutely love reading life coaching, self-help, and spiritual books that draw you into a deeper exploration of one's soul. Here are ten (10) books that speak to my "unique situation". Feel free to draw upon my book list, but I encourage you to explore your own unique journey through life and identify authors who speak to your spirit on how to make sense of your past and present life, in preparation for your future growth and development.

1. The Seat of the Soul *(Gary Zukav)*
2. The Four Agreements *(Don Miguel Ruiz)*
3. How to Stop Worrying and Start Living *(Dale Carnegie)*
4. The Positive Principle Today *(Norman Vincent Peale)*
5. The Road Less Travel *(Scott Peck)*
6. Mary Kay on People Management *(Mary Kay Ashe)*
7. The Value in the Valley: A Black Women's Guide through Life's Dilemmas *(Iyanla Vanzant)*
8. One Day My Soul Just Opened Up *(Iyanla Vanzant)*

9. Living Positively One Day at a Time *(Dr. Robert Schuller)*
10. Think and Grow Rich *(Napoleon Hill)*

Entrepreneurial testimonies. One of the greatest sources of inspiration is hearing the testimonies of how other entrepreneurs succeeded in traveling the road you are pursuing. I love reading biographies and autobiographies of entrepreneurs where I am especially drawn to their early lives. When I stumble upon a narrative of "growing up in chaos, utter dysfunction, or dire poverty," I tend to go deeper into their stories because I can personally identify with those types of environments. I also like to read about the times they failed by society's standards. My fascination with entrepreneurial testimonies has resulted in a collection of profiles of entrepreneurs from diverse industries, ethnicities, gender, socio-economic backgrounds, and nationalities. I am discovering a pattern among successful entrepreneurs where most: (1) are from working class families; (2) experienced trauma and drama at an early age; and (3) had a miracle moment that changed their lives forever. I have listed my top ten (10) picks for entrepreneurial stories that inspire me with a quote that clearly sums up their principles for success and, in my opinion, are rooted in their childhood experience that serves as strength for their entrepreneurial journey.

LIST 10 ENTREPRENURUAL STORIES THAT "FUEL" ME

1. **HOWARD D. SCHULTZ** *(Chairman and CEO of Starbucks)*

"Discipline"

"Grow with discipline. Balance intuition with rigor. Innovate around the core. Don't embrace the status quo. Find new ways to see. Never expect a silver bullet. Get your hands dirty. Listen with empathy and over communicate with transparency. Tell your story, refusing to let others define you. Use authentic experiences to inspire. Stick to your values, they are your foundation. Hold people accountable, but give them the tools to succeed. Make the tough choices; it's how you execute that counts. Be decisive in times of crisis. Be nimble. Find truth in trials and lessons in mistakes. Be responsible for what you see, hear, and do. Believe."

2. **OPRAH WINFREY** *(Talk Show Host, Producer)*

"Believe"

"I've come to believe that each of us has a personal calling that's as unique as a fingerprint - and that the best way to succeed is to discover what you love and then find a way to offer it to others in the form of service, working hard, and also allowing the energy of the universe to lead you."

3. **MARY KAY ASHE** *(Founder of Mary Kay Cosmetics International)*

"Perseverance"

"I had to leave my personal problems at home. So I was determined to always go in there with a smile. No matter how I felt."

"People"

"Everyone has an invisible sign hanging from their neck saying, 'Make me feel important.' Never forget this message when working with people."

"Purpose"

"We must have a theme, a goal, a purpose in our lives. If you don't know where you're aiming, you don't have a goal. My goal is to live my life in such a way that when I die, someone can say, she cared."

4. **TED TURNER** *(Founder of Cable News Network)*

"Vision"

"We won't be signing off until the world ends. We'll be on, and we will cover the end of the world, live, and that will be our last event . . . we'll play 'Nearer, My God, to Thee' before we sign off."

5. **STEVE JOBS** *(Co-founder of APPLE, Inc.)*

"Innovation"

"Sometimes when you innovate, you make mistakes. It is best to admit them quickly, and get on with improving your other innovations."

"Time Management"

"Your time is limited, don't waste it living someone else's life. Don't be trapped by dogma, which is living the result of other people's thinking. Don't let the noise of others' opinions drown your own inner voice. And most important, have the courage to follow your heart and intuition, they somehow already know what you truly want to become. Everything else is secondary."

6. **MADAME C.J. WALKER** *(Founder of Madame C.J. Walker Manufacturing Company)*

"Hard work"

"I am a woman who came from the cotton fields of the South. From there I was promoted to the washtub. From there I was promoted to the cook kitchen. And from there I promoted myself into the business of manufacturing hair goods and preparations. I have built my own factory on my own ground."

"Dream"

"One night I had a dream, and in that dream a big black man appeared to me and told me what to mix up for my hair. I made up my mind I would begin to sell it."

7. **TYLER PERRY** *(Filmmaker, producer, and director)*

"Confirmation"

"It doesn't matter if a million people tell you what you can't do, or if ten million tell you no. If you get one yes from God that's all you need."

"Connectivity"

"I've never chased money. It's always been about what I can do to motivate and inspire people."

8. **BERRY GORDY** *(Founder of Motown Record Label)*

"Process"

"Every day I watched how a bare metal frame rolling down the line would come out the other end a spanking brand new car. Maybe I could do the same thing with my music ... create a place where a kid off the street could walk in one door an unknown and come out another door a star."

"Street Smarts"

"Whenever I came up against presidents of other companies, I was always smarter, because I was from the streets."

9. **S. TRUETT CATHY** *(Founder of Chick-fil-A)*

"Confidence"

"No goal is too high if we climb with care and confidence."

"Prioritize"

"I'd like to be remembered as one who kept my priorities in the right order. We live in a changing world, but we need to be reminded that the important things have not changed, and the important things will not change if we keep our priorities in proper order."

"Self-Motivation"

"It is when we stop doing our best work that our enthusiasm for the job wanes. We must motivate ourselves to do our very best, and by our example lead others to do their best as well."

"Character"

"I believe no amount of business school training or work experience can teach what is ultimately a matter of personal character. Businesses are not dishonest or greedy, people are. Thus, a business, successful or not, is merely a reflection of the character of its leadership."

10. **STEVE HARVEY** *(Comedian, Television Host, Radio Personality, and Actor)*

"Gifted"

"Do not ignore your gift. Your gift is the thing you do the absolute BEST with the LEAST amount of effort."

"Fearless"

"The first step, I think, is to get over the fear of losing a man by confronting him. Just stop being afraid, already. The most successful people in this world recognize that taking chances to get what they want is much more productive than sitting around being too scared to take a shot. The same philosophy can be applied to dating: if putting your requirements on the table means you risk him walking away, it's a risk you have to take. Because that fear can trip you up every time; all too many of you let the guy get away with disrespecting you, putting in minimal effort and holding on to the commitment to you because you're afraid he's going to walk away and you'll be alone again. And we men? We recognize this and play on it, big time."

Listening pleasure. Authentic entrepreneurs take full responsibility for what music they listen to. I have a soundtrack for my entrepreneurial journey. I have songs for all occasions. I read motivational poems and spoken word as well. I have organized the songs I listen to by the chapter themes of this book. You can borrow from my soundtrack or use my approach to develop your own playlist. The goal is to take control of what goes into your ear gate, and ultimately penetrates your head and heart.

SONGS TO MOTIVATE YOU AS YOU SHIFT FROM A CAREER TO A CALLING

1. My Mind Is Made Up *(Rev. Milton Brunson & Thompson Community Singers)*
2. *Go Get It (Mary Mary)*
3. I Believe I Can Fly *(R. Kelly)*
4. Ease on Down the Road *(The Wiz Soundtrack)*
5. Boom Boom Pow *(The Black Eyed Peas)*
6. Black Butterfly *(Denise Williams)(Sounds of Blackness)*
7. Cantaloop *(Flip Fantasia)*
8. Green Light *(John Legend featuring Andre 3000)*
9. Put Your Hands Together *(O'Jays)*
10. Let's Get it Started *(M.C. Hammer)*

SONGS TO INSPIRE A HEALTHY FLOW OF AUTHENTIC ENTHUSIASM

1. Feeling Good *(Nina Simone) (Jennifer Hudson)*
2. One Moment in Time *(Whitney Houston)*
3. Be A Lovely Day *(Kirk Franklin and The Nu Nation Project) (Bill Withers)*
4. It's Time for the Motivator *(Dr. Quinn Motivates)*
5. I'm Every Woman *(Chaka Khan)(Whitney Houston)*
6. What a Feeling *(Irene Cara/Flash Dance Soundtrack)*
7. Smile *(Kirk Franklin)*
8. I Believe *(Fantasia)*
9. Be Encouraged *(William Becton & Friends)*
10. Get Up *(Mary Mary)*

SONGS TO INSPIRE YOU TO RE-PURPOSE YOUR PAST

1. Better *(Jessica Reedy)*
2. God Bless the Child *(Billie Holiday) (David Peaston) (Bubbling Brown Sugar Soundtrack)*
3. His Eyes is on the Sparrow *(Lauryn Hill; Tonya Blount/Sister Act 2 Soundtrack)(Bubbling Brown Sugar Soundtrack)(The Mississippi Children's Choir)*
4. Your Mercy *(Blessed)*
5. My Life *(Mary J. Blige)*
6. Clean Inside *(Hezekiah Walker)*
7. I Want to Know What Love is *(Foreigner)*
8. Wildflower *(New Birth) (The O'Jays)*
9. You Survived *(James Fortune and FIYA)*
10. I'm a Survivor *(Destiny's Child)*

SONGS TO MOTIVATE YOU AS YOU DEFINE YOUR BRAND

1. Expression *(Salt N Pepa)*
2. A Brand New Kind of Me *(Alicia Keys)*
3. Control *(Janet Jackson)*
4. Pieces of Me *(Ledisi)*
5. Express Yourself *(Charles Wright and the Watts 103rd Street Rhythm Band)*
6. Wake Up Everybody *(Harold Melvin & The Blue Notes)*
7. If You Believe *(Dee Dee Bridgewater/The Wiz Soundtrack)*
8. It Don't Mean a Thing *(Original Cast/Bubbling Brown Sugar Soundtrack)*
9. Give the People What They Want *(The O'Jays)*
10. I'm Not Your Average Girl *(India Arie)*

SONGS TO MOTIVATE YOU AS YOU BUILD YOUR BUSINESS MANAGEMENT SYSTEM

1. Encourage Yourself *(Donald Lawrence & the Tri-City Singers)*
2. God in Me *(Mary Mary)*
3. I Go to Work *(Kool Moe Dee)*
4. Working Day and Night *(Michael Jackson)*
5. Superwoman *(Alicia Keys)*
6. Run the World *(Beyoncé)*
7. Bad Mama Jama *(Carl Thomas)*
8. Roar *(Katie Perry)*
9. Empire State of Mind *(Jay-Z featuring Alicia Keys)*
10. I Got This *(Jennifer Hudson)*

SONGS TO INSPIRE YOU AS YOU BUILD YOUR DREAM TEAM

1. Love on Top *(Beyoncé)*
2. Work That *(Mary J. Blige)*
3. Bring 'Em Out *(T.I.)*
4. Wind Beneath my Wings *(Bette Midler) (Pattie Labelle)*
5. Lean on Me *(Bill Withers) (Club Nouveau)*
6. U.N.I.T.Y. *(Queen Latifah)*
7. I'll be There For You/You're All I Need to Get By *(Method Man featuring Mary J. Blige)*
8. Bonnie & Clyde *(Jay-Z featuring Beyoncé)*
9. I'll Take you There *(The Staple Singers)*
10. You're All I Need to Get By *(Marvin Gaye and Tamie Terrell)*

SONGS TO INSPIRE YOU DURING THE GROWTH AND MAINTENANCE PROCESSES

1. Everything Must Change *(Nina Simone) (George Benson) (Oleta Adams)*
2. For the Love of Money *(O'Jays)*
3. A Change is Gonna Come *(Sam Cooke)*
4. Ooh Child *(The Five Stair Steps) (Donnie McClurkin featuring Kirk Franklin)*
5. Fight the Power *(Isley Brothers) (Public Enemy)*
6. Money, That's What I Want *(Barrett Strong)*
7. Move on Up *(Curtis Mayfield)*
8. Hate on Me *(Jill Scott)*
9. This Girl is on Fire *(Alicia Keys)*
10. We Started from the Bottom Now We Hear *(Drake)*

SONGS TO INSPIRE YOU WHEN YOU FAIL BETTER

1. Stand *(Donnie McClurkin)*
2. Hello Fear *(Kirk Franklin)*
3. Still I Rise *(Yolanda Adams)*
4. Conqueror *(Estelle)*
5. Not the Time *(Marvin Sapp)*
6. Bridge over Troubled Water *(Aretha Franklin)*
7. This Means War *(Charles Jenkins)*
8. I Really Gotta Use My Imagination *(Gladys Knight and the Pimps)*
9. It Ain't Over... Until God Says It's Over *(Maurette Brown Clark)*
10. All I Do is Win *(DJ Khaled f/ T-Pain, Snoop Dogg, Rick Ross & Ludacris)*

SONGS TO MOTIVATE YOU AS YOU HONOR YOUR PRIORITIES

1. I Wish *(Steve Wonder)*
2. The Greatest Love of All *(George Benson) (Whitney Houston)*
3. Inseparable *(Natalie Cole)*
4. Never Would Have Made It *(Marvin Sapp)*
5. Do You Know Where You're Going To *(Diana Ross)*
6. Golden *(Jill Scott)*
7. On the Wings of Love *(Jeffrey Osborne)*
8. I Hope You Dance *(Gladys Knight) (Ronan Keating)*
9. Just Fine *(Mary J. Blige)*
10. Shake Your Tale Feather *(Ike & Tina Turner)*

SONGS TO MOTIVATE YOU TO PUNCH A CLOCK THAT NEVER STOPS

1. I Believe *(Fantasia)*
2. 99 and a Half *(Hezekiah Walker & The Love Fellowship Crusade Choir)*
3. Push It *(Salt & Pepa)*
4. Proud Mary *(Ike & Tina Turner)*
5. The Blessings of Abraham *(Donald Lawrence & The Tri-City Singers)*
6. Planet Rock *(Afrika Bambaataa & Soulsonic Force)*
7. Bankhead Bounce *(Diamond featuring D-Roc)*
8. Too Legit to Quit *(M.C. Hammer)*
9. Higher Ground *(Stevie Wonder)*
10. Ain't No Stopping Us Now *(McFadden & Whitehead)*

10 TED-TALKS TO INSPIRE ENTREPRENEURS

TED talks (technology, entertainment, design) is defined as a video created from a presentation on any topic for no more than 18 minutes and recorded at a TED conference or one of its many satellite events around the world. I became a fan of Ted-talks when I heard Brené Brown on Oprah's soul show. After listening to Oprah's interview, I searched for Brown and viewed her TED talk titled "The Power of Vulnerability." Of course after a few hours of surfing and listening I was hooked on the TED Talk brand. In fact, you might want to google TED talks because new ones on diverse topics are posted regularly. The ones I have listed below have been most inspiring during my entrepreneurial pursuit.

TED TALKS TO INSPIRE ENTREPRENEURS

1. How Great Leaders Inspire Action *(Simon Sinek)*
2. The Power of Vulnerability *(Brené Brown)*
3. Why We Do What We Do *(Tony Robbins)*
4. The Puzzle of Motivation *(Dan Pink)*
5. Your Elusive Creative Genius *(Elizabeth Gilbert)*
6. 5 Ways to Kill Your Dreams *(Bel Pesce)*
7. Women Entrepreneurs, Example Not Exception *(Gayle Tzemach Lemmon)*
8. Life at 30,000 Feet *(Richard Branson)*
9. How to Manage for Collective Creativity *(Linda Hill)*
10. How to Get Your Ideas to Spread *(Seth Godin)*

10 INSPIRATIONAL POEMS

1. It Couldn't be Done *(Edgar Guest)*
2. And Still I Rise *(Maya Angelou)*
3. Phenomenal Woman *(Maya Angelou)*
4. Choices *(Nicki Giovanni)*
5. The Road not Taken *(Robert Frost)*
6. Mother to Son *(Langston Hughes)*
7. If *(Rudyard Kipling)*
8. The Invitation *(Oriah Mountain Dreamer)*
9. If I Can Stop One Heart From Breaking *(Emily Dickerson)*
10. Lift Ev'ry Voice and Sing *(James Weldon Johnson)*

10 MOTIVATIONAL QUOTES

1. "Our <u>deepest</u> fear is not that we are inadequate. Our <u>deepest</u> fear is that we are powerful beyond measure. We often ask ourselves, Who am I to be brilliant, gorgeous, talented, fabulous? When in fact, you should be asking yourself, who are you <u>not</u> to be brilliant, gorgeous, talented, and fabulous?" *(Marianne Williamson, Author, Lecturer, and Spiritual Teacher)*

2. "Someone once told me not to bite off more than I could chew. I said I'd rather choke on greatness than nibble on mediocrity." *(Source Unknown)*

3. "I need you to know and embrace the power of one. You are more than enough." *(Judy Smith, Crisis Management Expert and Author)*

4. "Nothing Great was ever achieved without enthusiasm." *(Ralph Waldo Emerson, Essayist, Lecturer, and Poet)*

5. "Take what you do seriously, but yourself lightly." *(Ken Blanchard &*

10 MOTIVATIONAL QUOTES

Terry Waghman, Authors and Leadership Experts)

6. "Come to the edge, He said. They said, we are afraid. Come to the edge, He said. They came. He pushed them...and they flew." (*Guilliaume Apollinaire, French poet, Playwright, Novelist, and Art Critic*)

7. "God Bless the Child that got his own." (*Billie Holiday, Songwriter and Performer*)

8. "Never, Never, Never Give up." (*Winston Churchill, Prime Minister of Great Britain*)

9. "No one need fear death. We need fear only that we may die without having known our greatest power." (*Norman Cousins, Political journalist, Author, and Professor*)

10. "If it's hard, then do it hard." (*Les Brown, Author and Motivational Speaker*)

FIFTY MOVIES TO INSPIRE AND MOTIVATE ME TO STAY THE COURSE AND ACHIEVE AGAINST THE ODDS

1. Rudy
2. Diary Of A Mad Black Woman
3. The Untouchables
4. Fried Green Tomatoes
5. Beyond The Lights
6. The Color Purple
7. Waiting To Exhale
8. Brown Sugar
9. Just Wright
10. School Daze
11. Dream Girls
12. Deliver Us From Eva
26. Eve's Bayou
27. The Wiz
28. It's Complicated
29. The Apostle
30. Flash Dance
31. Set It Off
32. Lean On Me
33. In Pursuit Of Happiness
34. Head Of State
35. Mahogany
36. Two Can Play That Game
37. Love Jones

FIFTY MOVIES TO INSPIRE AND MOTIVATE ME TO STAY THE COURSE AND ACHIEVE AGAINST THE ODDS

13. The Associate
14. Flight
15. Akeila And The Bee
16. Down In The Delta
17. Talk To Me
18. A Chorus Line
19. Pay It Forward
20. Fame
21. Five Heart Beats
22. Soul Food
23. Something's Gotta Give
24. The Lion King
25. Love & Basketball
38. Forrest Gump
39. JOHN Q
40. Awakenings
41. What's Love Got To Do With It
42. The Devil Wears Prada
43. Annie
44. Philadelphia
45. The Negotiator
46. Bridesmaids
47. Mo Better Blues
48. Catch Me If You Can
49. Jungle Fever
50. The Temptations

MY "DRIVING" LESSONS LEARNED
IN FINDING MY HEALTHY FLOW OF ENTHUSIASM

1. **FAITH-BASED.** I committed whole-heartedly to operate out of faith in God. This resulted in my accepting the calling to ministry where I graduated from the Women's Institute of Ministry as a licensed minister in 2006.

2. **FELLOWSHIP.** I joined small group bible-studies at church. The ones that contributed the most to my entrepreneurial pursuit were: (1) The Purpose-driven life, (2) The Master Life Series, (3) The Disciple's prayer life, and (4) The Prayer of Jabez.

3. **FAVOR.** I cleared my conscience of "survivor's guilt" and "imposter syndrome," and replaced both with a renewed understanding of God's favor at work in my life.

4. **FRUITS OF THE SPRIT.** I found ways to apply the fruits of the spirit in my life to address character flaws as I pursued entrepreneurship in a carnal world.

5. **FORGIVENESS.** After fully understanding the principles governing forgiveness (grace and mercy), I forgave and asked for forgiveness from those that I caused pain as well.

6. **FEELINGS.** I learned to acknowledge my feelings (as opposed to suppress them) before they resulted in what I call "energy and enthusiasm killers," such as fear, anxiety, worry, guilt, and self-doubt.

7. **FLOW.** I learned to keep flowing through messy, confusing, muddy, and stormy processes associated with building business.

8. **FATIGUE.** There were times when I was just plain tired. Other times I was burned out and others I was depressed. I learned to acknowledge and accept the days that I simply need to rest and restore.

9. **FISCAL RESPONSIBILITY.** I realized that a lot of what was keeping me up at night and zapping my energy had to do with personal and business money management. I took full responsibility in both areas of financial management.

10. **FINISH STRONG.** As the creative leader of my firm, I had to learn the hard way that I must monitor quality and high standards of performance among all employees and teaming partners as a key step in finishing each project with excellence.

"The most empowering source of enthusiasm is in your response to why you do what you do. Not what you do and not how you do it… but the entrepreneurial magic is in the WHY you do it. And when it comes to entrepreneurship, the stronger the why, the longer the drive!"

Dr. Quinn Motivates

Now Let's Go!

CHAPTER 3
ARE YOU WILLING TO RE-PURPOSE YOUR PAST?
Never underestimate the power of your past struggles.

> *"While I have never been ashamed of my life story, I must say that until recently, I never really recognized the full power of my experiences."*
> Dr. Quinn Motivates

The inspiration for chapter three (3) titled "Are you willing to re-purpose your past" is based primarily on my working through Iyanla Vanzant's 40-day program called "One Day My Soul Just Opened Up." After reading Iyanla's work many times over, I developed a model designed to help creative high achievers unleash some suppressed experiences that are significant for authentic entrepreneurs as well. In order to re-purpose your past you must step outside yourself and examine the choices, forces, trauma, drama, missed-moments, mistakes, strengths, and struggles to determine how these experiences contribute to your entrepreneurial drive. As a way to guide individuals through this process, I developed a model for "Getting to the "HEART" of the Matter." It is designed as a journey through past and present realities, as well as a space for declaring what your heart desires for your future.

*So what does it take to get to the **HEART** of the matter as a strategy for ultimately re-purposing your past?*

DR. QUINN'S MODEL FOR "GETTING TO THE 'HEART' OF THE MATTER"				
H	E	A	R	T
HISTORY	EMOTIONS	ADDICTIONS	RELATIONSHIPS	TRANSFORMATION

In this chapter I provide a cursory introduction to the full curriculum on "Getting to the Heart of the Matter" as I believe it is an awesome tool for examining and re-purposing past life experiences for entrepreneurship. In keeping with the "DRIVE" model, think of "Getting to the Heart of the Matter" as synonymous with cleaning out the trunk of the car, checking the engine, and changing the tires to maximize the vehicle's performance.

HISTORY: How to Re-purpose Our "Past" to Stop Repeating It

The **H** in the acronym of "HEART" centers on the need to be at peace with your **HISTORY**. The work that needs to be done is to re-purpose your past so you can stop repeating it. Many of us are unable to move forward in life because we are in bondage to a past that has never been properly processed. A "properly processed" past entails a "truth-telling" journey of examining the people, places, periods in time, and the part you played in your past experiences. The key to the process is to understand who you are in a way that frees you from being defined by others. The journey to examining your **"PAST"** is to revisit the repeated messages and behaviors associated with your upbringing. Using an acronym for "PAST", open yourself to examine: (1) your interactions with your parents; (2) your growth and development during your adolescent years; (3) your interactions with siblings, and other social groups, including extended family, peers, team members, church groups, etc.; and (4) how you learned the virtues of trust and truth.

> **P** arents
> **A** dolescent Years
> **S** iblings and Social Groups
> **T** rust and Truth

Parents. One of the most painful, yet powerful undertakings in examining one's history is to take an empathic perspective on how you were parented. Your current actions, reactions, drive, or lack thereof, fears, risk-taking, etc. are all impacted by the kind of parents that had the responsibility of providing for, raising, nurturing, and supporting you. When doing this work, what I discovered is that no matter one's socio-economic status growing up, each person has some painful memories that need to be properly processed into a personal strength. There are four (4) primary parenting styles that shape our "rearing" and "upbringing." The best case scenario is to have caring adults that can synergize to provide the best of the strengths to be derived from each of the primary parenting styles summarized below.

The dominant parent. If you were reared by a primarily dominant parent, then you experienced high degrees of total management and full accountability in your household with very little tolerance for rule breaking and seemingly extreme punishment for even the most minor offenses. If you were anything less than overly ambitious, then you may have been traumatized by the dominant parent even though they meant well.

The influential parent. Those who grew up with influential parents faced the softer side of a dominant parent. By this I mean, the influential parent still wants to raise a high-achieving child, but they are not as hard on the child as the dominant parent. However, influential parents can flip the switch if you veer off the high-achievement course. Extroverted children who love to perform in public thrive well with influential parents. Introverted, more mechanical children may have been sidelined in such environments and internalized their parent's lack of attention as a form of abandonment or rejection.

The servant parent. Children raised by servant parents get the most nurturing of all. However, servant parents may not push their children to realize their full potential. Nevertheless, these parents are sensitive, patient, and great listeners. Introverted, shy, or only children fare well in this household because they feel very secure. Children who are outgoing and want to explore more risky activities and environments may have had problems with this parent's tendency to be over-protective.

The conscientious parent. The final parent is the conscientious parent. These are children who are raised by teachers, preachers, and perhaps politicians. These children are raised to be morally responsible and socially concerned, with lots of public rituals and appearances of the "good family." Their parents often are caring for others at the expense of their own children. Moreover, these children often hide the double life that is being lived where they may have a dysfunctional private life and a "Huxtables" public persona. Some of these children grow up very angry for having to live secrets and lies, and for having to share their parents with the public.

Dysfunctional parents. Within each of these general parental types, there may be various degrees of dysfunction. In re-purposing past experiences, you may be able to see where some painful experiences at the hands of dysfunctional and neglectful parents can be a strength in the entrepreneurial journey. An abbreviated list of the types of parents who struggle to provide optimal care, protection, and provision for their children include: (1) absentee parents; (2) substance-abusing and addicted parents (alcohol, drugs, gambling, sex, shopping, etc.); (3) workaholic parents; (4) cheating parents; (5) violent parents; (6) chronically-ill parents; (7) teen mothers; (8) high school drop-outs, (9) chronically unemployed parents; (10) chronically homeless parents; (11) overbearing/helicopter parent; (12) neglectful/inattentive parents; and (13) the best friend/boy husband parent.

If you were raised by a combination of one or more of the parents listed above, then it is highly likely that you experienced pain and trauma throughout your childhood. It is important to note that I did not list being raised in a single-parent home automatically as a dysfunction. This is because single parent homes can be some of the most well-organized, caring environments imaginable that create opportunities for young people to be leaders, more accountable, and responsible. However, if that single parent home also has some of the other issues on the list above, then there may be a need to properly process the way in which you were raised. At the same time, I have witnessed many two-parent households fail miserably at raising children as they try to live up to the ideal family in public while falling apart privately. In fact, one of the most common confessions among mothers in two-parent households is that they feel like they are living a lie and are actually, "married, but raising children as a single parent."

Adolescent years. As a life coach, I tend to inquire and probe more intensely about my adult clients' experiences during their adolescent years. I do so because this is the time that no matter one's parental situation, adolescents begin to develop a capacity to think and act and make decisions that profoundly shape who they become later in life. In applying my observations to one's entrepreneurial pursuit, I am hoping to discover untapped potential and talents, unwrapped gifts, and un-attempted goals and aspirations. Also I highlight ways in which adolescent experiences shaped one's overall concept of self. In like manner, I encourage you to spend some quality time reflecting upon your adolescent years and how different experiences serve as obstacles or opportunities for you to gain skills, values, ethics, and competencies that are typically associated with being an authentic entrepreneur.

Siblings and Social Groups. An individual's recollection of interactions with siblings and other social groups provides a wealth of insight into ones' capacity and willingness to aim for higher pursuits. In terms of entrepreneurship, it is important to examine how you learned creativity, cooperation, and competiveness. For example, accounts of sibling relationships provide indicators of what kind of team player or leader one might be later in life. In addition, youth tend to be part of two distinct types of social groups. First, they take part in social groups that are part of their extended family (primarily same-age cousins), neighbors, church peer affiliates, and the children of their parents' associates and friends. The second type of socializing among youth comes about through the activities they select to be part of, such as sports and dance teams, band, and other school-based clubs and activities. It also reveals a lot when young people are not part of any extra-curricular activities. In any case, the significance of groups is that typically, individuals use members of the group as benchmarks and references to aspire to. If you belong to a group dominated by over-achievers, then you tend to raise your game. If you interact in groups full of average performers, then you might settle for mediocre, or develop a false sense of achievement if you are a top performer on a second-rate team.

Truth and Trust. Truth and trust are necessary virtues in the entrepreneurial world. Without truth, you lack knowledge for sound decision-making. Without trust you are unable to partner and employ effectively. The problem with truth and trust is the ways in which one's socializing agents introduce them. Take the time to sort through mixed messages and images of what you learned as definitions and examples of "truth" and "trust". What I discovered in my work as a behavioral scientist is that most people are afraid to conduct an independent investigation of the truth about who we are because: (1) we don't want to even remotely consider that those who cared for us may have lied to us; and (2) we really don't want the responsibility of acting on the truth that is different from the lies we have grown accustomed to accommodating and the secrets we have learned to hide so well.

EMOTIONS: NAMING THE PAIN AND NUMBING PROCESS

The **E** in the acronym of "HEART" addresses the underlying negative **EMOTIONS** that keep you from moving forward. When entrepreneurs are bogged down in negative emotions rooted in a painful past, they tend to lack emotional intelligence in their decision-making process and their interactions with sub-ordinate associates in particular. When you are negatively impacted by past emotions, it manifests in your entrepreneurial experiences as you hide behind the mask of the position of CEO. In your leadership role, some examples that signal deep-seated emotional damage include intentionally withholding information others need to do a good job, intimidating others, becoming a control freak, and shutting down the feedback process to avoid hearing how your behaviors are negatively impacting others.

There are five (5) negative emotions shaped primarily by past painful experiences that tend to manifest at the most inopportune moments in your pursuit of entrepreneurship. These negative emotions include: (1) anger; (2) fear; (3) shame; (4) guilt; and (5) sadness. As you unpack what triggers one or more of these negative emotions, it is important to see them as the very issues that have limited your ability to grow as an authentic entrepreneur.

Fear. Fear manifests when you lack trust and truth about who you are and what the future entails. Most fears stem from childhood and spillover into your adult years. For example, if you were raised by a dominant parent, you learn to fear failure. If you were raised by an influential parent, you tend to fear rejection and not being liked. Those raised by servant parents fear loss of security; while those raised by conscientious parents fear change and instability.

No matter the source of fear, rather than deal with it, most learn to disguise fear. For example, if you fear losing control, you micromanage or prolong decision-making. Those who fear failure, tend to think of creative ways to blame others when they fall short of their goals. Closely related, those who fear that they are inadequate, are inclined to sabotage significant relationships as they don't feel worthy of the connection. The list could go on and on, but the bottom line is that, without the appropriate intervention and redirection, most tend to find more clever ways to protect themselves from that which they fear.

Shame. Shame is feeling bad about who you are, how you look, and things that you have done. Just as with fear, the things we are most ashamed of tend to take root in our childhood. The most devastating forms of shame are those tied to being exploited and abused as a child. When not properly healed, those experiencing "chronic shame" protect that wounded child by any means necessary. Some ways in which suppressed issues of shame manifest later in adults, and thus have implications for entrepreneurs include: (1) losing hope about the future; (2) altering one's perception of "goodness;" (3) creating a sense of powerlessness; (4) self-sabotaging; (5) feeling unworthy of love and unwelcomed; (6) distrustful; and (7) lacking security in the environments within one functions. When shame is not properly processed, individuals tend to live a life of secrecy and avoidance of intense emotional attachment to significant others.

Guilt. Guilt is judging oneself based upon something you believe or how you behave. In fact, Iyanla Vanzant often calls guilt "the most wasted of all emotions". Guilt and shame work together in doing maximum damage as shame says that there is something wrong with me, while guilt says that there is something wrong with what I have done. Guilt can be functional as it alerts your soul that you have said or done something for which you should be remorseful. However, most suffer from "toxic guilt" that sets in after you have apologized, made amends to the extent possible, but you still have a lingering guilty conscious. Others suffer from "survivor's guilt" where they succeed or survive against the odds when others fail or lose their lives. You don't quite know how to feel about the fact that you were the one who made it out alive when many died, or that you are thriving when others are suffering. Some tend to grant "guilt gifts" to over-compensate or over-correct for things you believe are wrong, whether you caused them or not.

Also, be mindful that others can send you on a "guilt trip" where, even after you have acknowledged you may have caused them problems, they find ways to keep making you pay for the same mistake. Then there is "imposter's guilt" where you believe you have not earned the success you have so you either shrink or keep striving for more accolades to prove your worth. Until you make peace with that which causes you to feel guilty, you will never fully achieve that which you are capable because prolonged guilt serves as a repeat form of self-punishment.

Anger. Anger is best defined as an explosive response to built-up frustration. We are especially explosive if we believe that our personal power has been violated.   As it is not everyone's nature to explode in the typical fashion we are accustomed to seeing anger expressed, some use proxies for "anger" that are more passive-aggressive, such as resentment, self-pity, depression, jealousy, anxiety, or stress.

In any case, the seeds of anger stemming from childhood are often associated with having been abandoned, abused, and neglected. Others have a sense of entitlement and become angry when they are deprived of having their way. Another source of anger is constantly comparing yourself to others and feeling envious or jealousy. Finally, for many reasons, there is a lot of anger that comes from being in intimate relationships, including being lied to and cheated on. Some find ways to use their anger to fight injustices done to them and to others. Unfortunately, the darkest side of anger is when it results in violence. To be clear, anger is not always lashing out, but sometimes it is held internally and released in very passive-aggressive behavior. No matter its shape or form, anger is a poison that actually kills your spirit and zest for life.

Sadness. Sadness is characterized as emotional pain typically associated with feelings of loss, despair, helplessness, and sorrow. To be clear, short periods of sadness can be a healthy expression of disappointment or loss. However, prolonged sadness may lead to some people experiencing clinical levels of depression that may be caused by chemical imbalances in the brain. Still others have sadness that is part of their personality or temperament. Sometimes events and encounters can trigger memories of past experiences that result in sadness. Sadness can also signal depression and deep-seated hurts that have never been properly dealt with. As an authentic entrepreneur, it is imperative that you address any lingering issues of sadness that may hinder your ability to motivate and inspire key stakeholders to take this entrepreneurial journey with you.

In general, it is a very healthy and worthwhile process to work through the underlying issues that trigger negative emotions. No matter the negative emotion that rears its ugly head in your life, the healing processes are similar. For most, emotional stability can begin with simply changing the way you respond to people and situations that tend to trigger fear, shame, guilt, anger, and sadness. For some, however, the emotional damage can be so severe, that there may be a need for clinical care and therapy. At the extreme, should one be diagnosed with a chemical imbalance that causes mood swings, then psychiatric care and medication may be the best option for stabilizing one's emotions.

When pursuing a "self-help" approach to addressing the impact of negative emotions, keep in mind that the work that needs to be done is way more complex and comprehensive than just "don't do that" or "don't think that way" or "don't dwell on those things." Through a very rigorous process it is possible to re-purpose memories that trigger negative emotions and replace them with more "fruitful" feelings. Using the nine (9) "fruits of the spirit," it is possible to transfer every negative emotion to a more healthy feeling and outlook on even the most traumatizing life experiences.

Love. If you find yourself constantly responding to situations with the extremes of either, anger or sadness, it is a sign that you are not in a healthy relationship. You have two options. Do the work to get it to a healthy state, which requires all parties to be fully committed to resolving the issue, or you can apply "agape love" and learn to love some people from a healthy distance.

Joy. Anger and sadness will need to be replaced with a disposition of learning to rejoice in any situation. Clearly, none of us are exempt from an instinctive response of anger and sadness when we hear bad news or experience injustice in particular. However, when you spend time immersing yourself in a deeper level of serenity, you are able to draw strength from the Divine that all things that once made you angry or sad now produce joy.

Peace. Fear, guilt, and shame produce anxiety and keep conflicts going at multiple levels. To alleviate chronic guilt and shame you will need to rely upon a spiritual peace that only comes about through a relationship with God. This degree of peace renders you no longer afraid. Also, if you have resolved the things that left you feeling guilty, peace frees you from being held hostage by those who refuse to let the issue go. Finally, shame is addressed by acquiring an internal peace that whispers to you that you are whole, complete, and more than enough without needing approval from anyone.

Patience. Anger is often sparked by being impatient. As an entrepreneur, you will need to master the art of "waiting" as this virtue does not come easy when your money, time, and other resources are invested in an enterprise that needs to produce a profit. Patience includes the concepts of forbearance, long-suffering, and the willingness to bear wrongs patiently. Patience is not passive complacency, but is rather a hopeful fortitude that actively resists defeat. Patience also entails refraining from desperate measures to make things happen.

Kindness. Kindness is doing something good for someone and not expecting anything in return. Many times anger is displaced where you may be "lashing out" when you really need to "reach out" in a spirit of being kind, regardless if the person in question is deserving of such gestures. Reaching out to others to have a civil conversation, or restore bad relationships can work wonders to reduce anger. Also when you are sad, being good to others in words and deed can produce gladness. Be sure that your acts of kindness have the right motive. Many in entrepreneurship fear that their kindness will be taken for granted or as a sign of weakness, or even seen as a savvy action to get something in return.

Goodness. Closely related to kindness is goodness. Goodness is learning to live generously with your emotions. A spirit of goodness frees you from being an emotional hostage. Goodness results in your being able to forgive, grant grace and mercy in response to those who have spitefully used you, and demonstrate that at your very core you wish good and not evil upon those who have done you wrong.

Faithfulness. Faithfulness is committing to something or someone even if they have not made the same commitment to you. One of the greatest fears among entrepreneurs is that those you depend upon will let you down when their actions matters the most. This implies you lack the virtue of faithfulness. To examine why you lack faith, recall how you learned about "trust and truth." If you have been socialized in environments where individuals can't be trusted, then you are limited in your capacity for faithfulness. The work to be done to live a life of faithfulness is to be really selective on who you allow into your intimate space. You must develop a bottom line set of criteria for who can be in your inner-circle of the "faithful" few, and who can observe you from the "front pew."

Gentleness. Gentleness is conceptualized as the strength of being tender. This means that you are even-tempered under the worse conditions. This is not to be confused with being boiling hot and mad on the inside, but displaying calm externally. It is truly a tranquil, balanced spirit, both, inside and out, and even under fire. Gentleness will address the extreme emotions of being outraged to the extent you lash out or seek revenge. When you operate with a gentle spirit, you are able to render justice in a way that corrects faulty behavior without inflicting unnecessary harm to the person exhibiting the behavior.

Self-control. The way to control all of the negative emotions is to master your passions. Learn to control your temper. Winning the battle of self-control begins with facing the "inner-me" before attacking the external "enemy." Self-control is a form of self-awareness where you do the work to control your thoughts and actions.

ADDICTIONS: ADDRESS ANY ADDICTIONS

In our society we have been socialized to minimize pain and maximize pleasure. Over time pain management can evolve into an addiction. What's even more pronounced is how we conveniently separate "good" and "bad" addictions. In fact, we have constructed a vibrant recovery community around socially-unacceptable addictions such as illicit drugs, alcohol, sex, shopping, eating, or gambling. Because of the complicated nature of diagnosing and treating addictions, I am limited to a thesis of raising awareness that addictions include any behaviors used as a substitute to minimize pain over longer periods of time.

In an attempt to minimize pain and maximize pleasure, a number of socially-acceptable behaviors can become addictions.

These addictions that are socially acceptable may include, but are not limited to: (1) shopping; (2) technology; (3) social media; (4) romance; (5) multiple relationships; (6) power tripping and controlling; (7) religiosity; (8) community service; (9) working; (10) partying; (11) pathological lying; (12) over-protection of own children; (13) underachieving; and (14) over-achieving just to name a few that you would not normally label as "addictive behaviors."

Some individuals attempt to suppress painful emotions using another category of pain numbing behaviors. These behaviors are referred to as "maladaptive behaviors" where individuals display dysfunctional inter-personal responses to otherwise "normal' interactions. These pain numbing behaviors include: (1) defensive or rigid reactions; (2) denial and blaming; (3) aloofness and avoidance; and (4) detachment and uncaring.

The recovery process for all self-defeating behaviors entails the same humbling steps to regain power and control over one's thoughts, feelings, and actions. Most can rely upon non-clinical strategies to address the causes and consequences associated with minimizing pain. Do not be ashamed if you need clinical therapeutic care and legally prescribed and managed medication to address chemical imbalances in the brain that cause mood swings and disorders.

	STEPS FOR ADDRESSING ADDICTIVE BEHAVIORS
STEP 1	Admit that you are powerless over self-defeating behavior that you are using to numb or avoid pain.
STEP 2	Intensify your relationship with God.
STEP 3	Make a decision to become fully dependent upon God for care and comfort.
STEP 4	Identify moral and character flaws that are causes and consequences of your compulsive lifestyle.
STEP 5	Be transparent about the hurt, harm, and danger you have caused in your attempt to numb your own pain.

	STEPS FOR ADDRESSING ADDICTIVE BEHAVIORS
STEP 6	Be entirely ready to have God remove character flaws you identified in step four.
STEP 7	Humbly ask God to remove your shortcomings.
STEP 8	Put a name and nature on the harm you caused others.
STEP 9	Make attempts to make amends for the wrong you caused others, unless you perceive that to do so will injure that person.
STEP 10	Continue to engage in self-awareness and make changes and adjustments as you discover behaviors that are detrimental to yourself and others.
STEP 11	Commit to a life of prayer and meditation to guard against relapse.
STEP 12	Share your story.

RELATIONSHIPS: RETHINKING ALL RELATIONSHIPS

The **R** in the acronym of "HEART" requires you to think critically about your key relationships. There are at least five (5) types of relationships you need to consider as you commit to getting to the heart of the matters that impact your life: (1) your relationship with God; (2) your relationship with yourself; (3) your relationship with family and friends; (4) your relationships with business associates, partners, and employees; and (5) your relationship with intimate/sexual partner (s). The work in this area consists of literally writing out the names of everyone who fits any of the categories that you interact with on a daily, weekly, and even monthly basis. If the relationship is genuinely healthy, mutually beneficial, and not causing you any problems then check them off the list. However, if your spirit is grieved as you come across certain names, you should work through the "RELATE" model to get more clarity on what you are really feeling and why. After examining every important relationship through the "RELATE" model, it is your responsibility to act on the answers revealed to you.

		DR. QUINN'S "RELATE" MODEL FOR EXAMINING IMPORTANT RELATIONSHIPS
R	REALITY	• Write out in detail the current state of the relationship. • Write out in detail all the factors that you believe contributed to the relationship being in its current state of rift, dysfunction, or conflict.
E	EMOTIONS	• Determine how the relationship in question triggers negative emotional responses past and present: (1) anger, (2) fear, (3) shame, (4) guilt, and (5) sadness. • Determine the extent to which, when interacting with or thinking about a particular person, you believe it is possible to respond with one or more "fruitful responses" including: (1) love, (2) joy, (3) peace, (4) patience, (5) kindness, (6) goodness, (7) faithfulness, (8) gentleness, and (9) self-control.
L	LIKEABILITY FACTOR	• Answer the following question with vulnerability and transparency: "Do I really like this person in my space or am I just tolerating them to keep the peace or to avoid changes that are long overdue?"
A	ASPIRATIONS	• Within the context of my aspirations as an authentic entrepreneur, is this someone that can grow with me as I build my business?
T	TRUTH AND TRUST	• What "truth" do I really need to own when it comes to this particular person in my life? • Can I trust the divine working through him or her for the good? • Can I trust this person with my business?
E	ENRICHMENT	• What needs to be done to strengthen, revitalize, or show value in this relationship? • Does this relationship bring me fulfilment in one or more of the following areas as appropriate: (1) physical, (2) emotional, (3) financial, (4) spiritual, (5) recreational, (6) social, or (7) sexual intimacy?

TRANSFORMATION: TAKE ACTION PHASE. While you cannot change the past, never underestimate your power to re-purpose every pain, hurt, and struggle as resilience and strength for your future. The ultimate purpose of "Getting to the Heart of the Matter" is to make the necessary changes to live your best life. For the authentic entrepreneur, I use the "CHANGE" model as a way to process all that you experienced in the first four aspects of examining your history, emotions, addictions, and relationships. Now it is time to document that which you choose to "CHANGE".

	DR. QUINN'S "CHANGE" MODEL FOR TRANSFORMATION	
C	COMMITMENT	• What changes do you need to make in terms of the things you are committed to in relation to your pursuit of entrepreneurship?
H	HEALING	• Do you need to seek help for healing old hurts and wounds that hinder you from moving forward?
A	ACCEPT	• In examining the diverse people in your life, what do you need to finally accept about who they really are and what they mean to you?
N	NURTURE	• Going forward, what is your plan for accepting full responsibility for nurturing yourself as a way to forgive and release those who fail(ed) to provide proper emotional support, physical safety, and basic provision?
G	GOAL SET	• What stretch goals are you willing to set to unleash your entrepreneurial spirit in a way that reflects being released from past brokenness and bondage? • What is your plan for being bold, courageous, and radical towards achieving your stretch goals?
E	EMPOWERMENT	• What is your plan for exhibiting self-empowerment in all that you are capable of achieving as an authentic entrepreneur?

MY "DRIVING" LESSONS LEARNED
IN RE-PURPOSING MY PAST

1. **PAIN-RELEASE.** I invested in the emotional process of reflecting upon the people, places, and things that once caused me the most pain and anxiety. I re-purposed all the negativity I endured as "resilience".

2. **PERSPECTIVE.** I released from blame adults in my life that abandoned and rejected me as a child. I focused instead on the connections made along the way with caring adults at key times in my growth and development.

3. **PRODUCTIVITY.** The one quality I inherited from women on both sides of my family was "work-ethic." I learned that no matter the job, if I sign up, then I must show up. If I show up, then I need to find a way to stand out by going beyond the call of duty.

4. **PROTECTION.** Growing up with humble beginnings, I knew that no one was responsible for bailing me out of any financial jam and that it was my responsibility to protect my future by creating a financial safety plan and calling that "financial ground zero."

5. **POSSIBILITY-THINKING.** My life history is full of narratives of how I had to become a possibility thinker to compete with those from more affluent families. These early lessons in coping with being disadvantaged were key in applying the principles of possibility thinking to build my business.

6. **PROFITS.** Having grown up in an environment where the norm was living pay check to pay check, I had to process what it meant to make and keep money, and manage it strategically.

7. **PROVISION.** During difficult times over the course of my entrepreneurial growth, I drew upon early life lessons in self-sufficiency and self-reliance to accomplish my goals.

8. **PEN AND PAPER.** My past is full of evidence that I am a gifted writer with a diverse range in terms of subject matter and audiences.

9. **PASSION.** I found a way to profit from the activities that have brought me joy since childhood, which include: researching, writing, thinking, coaching, motivating, directing, leading, planning, and creating.

10. **PERSEVERE.** No matter what goes wrong the show must go on in assuring that my purpose-driven life remained on track.

"You don't have to hurt or harm anyone in your quest to re-purpose your past."

Dr. Quinn Motivates

Now Let's Go!

Chapter 4
Do you have a Clearly Defined Brand?
Before you can sell "it" you must sell "you."

"Your 'I' and 'Why' stories are central in moving your product or services from commodities to a brand."

Dr. Quinn Motivates

This chapter serves as a "crash course" on how to build a brand management system using traditional principles of marketing. As a former marketing executive for Fortune 100 companies, I am a firm believer that new entrepreneurs must immerse themselves in the fundamentals of traditional brand management. By investing in a rigorous and robust brand management system, your product or service has a better chance of surviving economic hardships and defending against fierce competition. In conducting workshops on brand management I have discovered that so many entrepreneurs have confused having a strong social media presence as synonymous with brand management. Social media is a necessary communications tool in today's marketplace, and it is an important vehicle for building brand awareness, however, social media is not a comprehensive brand management platform. Just like any other tool, social media has to be used properly to get the most effective results.

Authentic entrepreneurs should view branding as weaving your "who, what, how, why, and I" stories. In general, selling a product or service is a commodity. It is your brand management plan that separates your uniqueness and creates demand for the specific features and benefits you bring alive in your brand strategy. In re-working traditional brand management principles, I have devised a "BRAND" management program, which is more useful for entrepreneurs in the start-up and growth phases. It is explained below as I discuss branding in five (5) distinct phases: (1) brand name; (2) recognition; (3) attributes; (4) nurture; and (5) demand.

| DR. QUINN'S "BRAND" MANAGEMENT MODEL AT A GLANCE ||||||
B	R	A	N	D
Brand Name	Recognition	Attributes	Nurture	Demand

1. ESTABLISH A BRAND NAME

What are you going to name your firm in general and what do you name the various products and services you develop within the company? At this point, you should have a product or service in mind that you believe is marketable. In the conceptual phase, you have what is referred to as a "commodity." It is your responsibility to add benefits, features, bells, and whistles that serves as the "branding" of your basic product or service and sets you apart from competitors in the marketplace. Establishing and building a brand name as a first step signals to the industry that you have entered the market with a new product or service. You must establish and build a clear and concise brand name that communicates who and what you are in the marketplace. There are five (5) key factors to keep in mind in conceptualizing your company's name, and perhaps future sub-brands as well:

1. Your brand name should communicate a complex message rather quickly.
2. Your brand name should reflect your mission, vision, and overall purpose for doing what you do every day.
3. Your brand name should result in some emotional impact that sets the wheels in motion for attracting those that see the value in your brand.
4. Your brand name should evoke people to want to know the back story or the founder's "I" story.
5. Your brand name should serve as an easy segue' into your elevator pitch.

Once you have conceptualized these fundamental elements comprising a brand name, you should move into the mechanics of testing out various company names and related sub-branding ideas. Many people make the mistake of trying to develop symbols and logos at this stage. I do not recommend doing that because your brand name needs to be able to stand alone. At a minimum, create some sketches but don't commit to a logo until you work through the full brand management plan. Just remember that logos and other supporting tools change, but the company name needs to be solid and not overly reliant upon a logo to carry the brand name.

2. BUILD BRAND RECOGNITION

Brand recognition is built in two very distinct ways. First, *brand identity* is what brand owners do to set the stage for helping potential customers recognize the brand in the marketplace amidst competing options. Brand identity is how the entrepreneur wants people to define and internalize the brand. Second, *brand image* is how the customer or client actually defines your brand based on their own assessment and utilization. The key to brand recognition is the entrepreneur's role in bridging the gap between brand identity and brand image.

BRAND IDENTITY. Brand identity stems from the entrepreneur's responsibility for creating a distinguished product with unique characteristics. In establishing your brand identity, you need to think comprehensively about how you want to be perceived in the core markets you will enter on three (3) levels:

1. What you do (commodity)
2. How you do it (the mechanics)
3. Why you do it (purpose, mission, and vision)

Once you have conceptually framed these, then you are ready to think about building a brand identity. There are at least seven (7) distinct elements to consider when strategizing towards your brand identity: These core elements include: (1) vision; (2) culture; (3) positioning; (4) personality; (5) relationships; (6) presentation; and (7) symbols and logos.

1. **VISION.** The brand's vision is written in such a way to inspire and energize diverse stakeholders to see the big picture of where the brand

is headed. It includes the brand's core values, growth strategies, and defines what brand success looks like in the future.

2. **CULTURE.** A brand's culture takes shape as people relate to it based on their own values, customs, and traditions. Ultimately you want to create a "cult-like" following for your brand because these individuals become fantastic fans helping you spread the brand story based on their experiences.

3. **POSITIONING.** Brand positioning implies you know your core group of consumers and you are now preparing to put your products or services in places where they work, live, play, learn, and shop. Once you locate them in their natural environments, you must have a strategy for helping them quickly recognize your product or service as one that adds value to their lives or solves a problem. You want to create a brand positioning statement that communicates to the customer "why they should buy your product or services given other options."

4. **PERSONALITY.** Brand personality is giving your brand human-like characteristics. Just like an actual person, the brand's personality embodies its tone, mood, style, attitude, and visual disposition. Study recognizable brand personalities to give you an idea of how to develop one for your product or service. For example, my brand personality is "empowerment" and "high achievement." The Dove brand's personality is being feminist and optimistic. Hewlett Packard represents accomplishment and competency. BMW is known as the ultimate driving machine and resonates among risk takers. Some business owners become their own brand personality, such as Tyler Perry Studios, Mary Kay Cosmetics, or Oprah Winfrey's OWN Network. Other brands select trustworthy celebrities whose personality is synonymous with the brand's personality. In fact, I created "Dr. Quinn Motivates" as a way to be my brand's spokesperson. The catch is the customer has to believe the spokesperson actually uses the product or service. The risk is if the spokesperson faces some life-changing scandal or becomes a public relations nightmare, then it reflects negatively upon a brand's identity.

5. **RELATIONSHIPS.** A brand relationship is the relationship that consumers, think, feel, and have with a **brand**. Brand relationships are typically associated with "lifestyle brands" centered on fun, entertainment, and living life to the fullest. Examples of lifestyle brands include travel groups, theme party enthusiasts, family vacation destinations, and spa package retreats. When you embrace the concept of building a brand relationship, you want to focus on brand strategies that result in "fantastic fans." Not only do fantastic fans tend to repeat purchase, they become so enthusiastic about their experiences they share their stories, photos, and readily invite others to participate in future events. In essence, the personal relationships you have with fantastic fans permeate through their networks via "word of mouth" marketing. Over time, you create a community of people who are passionate about the product or service and can't wait to see what you create next.

6. **PRESENTATION.** Brand presentations are the marketing efforts employed to move the brand from "theory to practice" in creating a consistent and cohesive message across all the places and systems consumers interact with your brand. The brand's overall presentation should reflect your pre-determined goals for the products and services in the marketplace. In its simplest form, the brand's presentation is your core message or elevator speech. In its more complex platform, your brand's presentation is represented in your brand's reputation, direct and indirect associations, employee engagement, contributions to community and non-profits, as well as your personal presentation as the "CEO."

7. **SYMBOLS AND LOGOS.** Symbols and logos help customers remember your products and services. Once your brand reaches a level of maturity, you should be able to display your symbols and logos without mentioning the firm's name and you will still be recognized in the industry. This is why selecting a name that transcends fads is vital to your branding process. When deciding on your brand's symbols and logos, ask yourself these questions:

1. Have I unnecessarily complicated the image?
2. Am I sending too many symbolic messages in one image?
3. Is it uniquely different from a symbol/logo others use in my industry?
4. Will I be able to use this symbol/logo in developing my marketing and sales communications materials
5. What impact do I envision my symbols/logo will have on the intended audience?
6. Will my audience remember my symbol or logo?
7. What will be my color scheme?
8. Are my symbol and logo designs a perfect reflection of my firm?
9. What does my symbol/logo communicate about my company's values, vision, mission, or business objectives?
10. Do I want my logo to be a name type, an iconic visual, or a slogan?
11. Is my symbol/logo eligible for a trademark in terms of its degree of originality?

BRAND IMAGE. No matter the work done by the entrepreneur to establish a strong brand identity, it is the brand's image that ultimately matters. A brand's image primarily is shaped by the client's viewpoint of the product or service. This is why consumer research and interaction is vital in monitoring the brand's image and evaluating customer satisfaction. It is your responsibility to use consumer perspectives to align the brand identity with the brand's image. In monitoring and evaluating your brand's image, you want to answer the following questions:

1. What do customers think, feel, and expect when using my brand?
2. Are there particular features and benefits (functional and emotional) they discuss?
3. Are there particular experiences that could cost my brand its reputation?
4. Do my employees and other business associates feel proud of the brand?
5. Is my brand identity and brand image consistent or are there points of conflict?

6. Are there changes that need to be made to my marketing mix to bridge the gap between my intended brand identity and the brand image that resonates with the customer?

3. DELIVER ON YOUR BRAND ATTRIBUTES

The **A** in Brand is for "Brand Attributes." Brand attributes are what your brand promises to deliver consistently as highlighted in its features and benefits. Below are aspects to think through as you seek to build a communications plan for informing your target audience of your brand's attribute.

SEVEN (7) ASPECTS OF A SOLID BRAND ATTRIBUTES

1. **RELEVANCY.** The attributes you communicate must be relevant. Relevant means that the consumer can relate to the core message. Focus on those features and benefits that meet customers' expectations and will keep them coming back for future purchases.
2. **CONSISTENCY.** A brand is deemed consistent over time as key features and benefits come to be trusted as having delivered on what you claim they will do in the lives of customers. Think about the aspects of your products or services that the customer can depend upon to be consistent under all conditions.
3. **PROPER POSITIONING.** A strong brand should be positioned so that it is at the top of your target audience's mind when they think about addressing the problem your product or service promises to solve in the lives of customers.
4. **SUSTAINABLE.** A strong brand maintains its key features and benefits even as it undergoes intense growth phases to remain innovative, defends against fierce competition in the marketplace, or implements survival strategies during economic down turns.
5. **CREDIBILITY.** A strong brand builds credibility in the eyes of the customers, as they judge it to do what it promises. This is why it is so important to be realistic and not exaggerate about your brand's key features and benefits. Remember the customer gets to comment

publicly on their experience in using your product or service. Today's social media platforms give them an instant outlet for sharing their experiences, which can be a blessing or a curse depending upon what customers choose to share. I suggest monitoring social media to build upon great testimonials, but to also learn from less than flattering comments. Finally, be appropriately responsive should you discover half-truths, lies, or malicious reputation assassination being shared on social media or word of mouth as it is your responsibility to defend your brand's credibility under these conditions.

6. **INSPIRATIONAL.** Determine how to communicate key features and benefits in such a way that influences changes people want to make in their lives. For example, Nike's "just do it" slogan is matched with a comprehensive line of athletic wear highlighting the key features and benefits that result in high performance once the customer commits to "just do" whatever it takes to achieve her physical goals in the sport of her choice.

7. **UNIQUENESS.** A strong brand should set your product or service apart from other competitors in the marketplace.

4. NURTURE YOUR BRAND

Your products or services must be managed through a process I refer to as "nurturing your brand." I call it nurturing because you must come to see your brand as a baby needing nourishment, special care, and attention to give the brand a firm foundation from which to grow stronger and expand over time. Entrepreneurs must expand upon the traditional "4 Ps" of marketing management (product or service, place, price, and promotion). In thinking about a comprehensive approach to nurturing your brand, you must master "the 12Ps of brand management for entrepreneurs, which transcends the traditional 4Ps of marketing.

12 PS OF BRAND MANAGEMENT FOR ENTREPRENEURS AT A GLANCE

1. *Product or Service.* What does the customer want or need from your product or service (features, benefit)? What problems are you solving for the customer?" How is your product or service unique from the competition?

2. *Place.* Where are you going to physically place your product or service in the marketplace? Where do your consumers look for your products and service? What is your plan to access the right channels of distribution? What is your sales strategy for each distinct distribution channel?

3. *Price.* What is the value proposition of your product or service? How much does it cost you to make the product or administer the service being offered? How much money will you make selling the product at various price points? How price sensitive is your customer?

4. *Promotion.* What is your plan to reach and engage audiences in your marketing message? What is your budget for promotions? How will you involve your "fantastic fans," meaning those individuals who really believe in you and your business, to serve as spokespersons based upon their personal experience with your brand? How will you take advantage of "built environments" and "seasons"? For example, if your business is in the health and fitness industry, how do you take advantage of the fact that people tend to set wellness goals at the start of a new year? If your business is in youth development, how do you take advantage of the end or start of a new school year when parents are most sensitive to enrichment opportunities?

5. *Production.* What is the critical path along your production cycle, including access to raw materials, delivery time, human resource issues, storage, shipping and handling, and troubleshooting? What does it cost you to produce or manufacture your product? Have you explored and compared multiple production options, including a back-up production plan if it becomes necessary? How will you produce it and what does it cost you to produce it.

6. *Packaging.* What is your packaging design plan? Does your packaging option protect the product from damage? How much does it cost to package your product? Is the packaging compatible with your overall brand message?

7. *Partnerships.* What partnerships do you need to help build and expand the brand? Do your partners understand your brand and vision? What formal agreement is in place to assure that all partners understand key deliverables, timing, quality, and payment? Is there inherent trust and open communications with all key partners? Is there a non-compete clause in your partnership agreement?

8. *Project management.* Have you mastered the continuum of "big-picture" to "details?" What needs to happen on an annual, quarterly, monthly, weekly, and even daily basis to execute your brand with excellence? Have the core elements of project management been articulated to all team members in writing? Is there a qualified person serving in the role of project manager?

9. *People management.* What is your plan for managing people along the continuum responsible for key aspects of the brand? What is your budget for paying people? How much time have you set aside for engaging people who work on your brand in diverse capacities?

10. *Probing.* What time do you set aside to immerse yourself in the industry within which your business operates? What is your strategy for consumer engagement to understand needs and buying behavior of diverse sub-segments? How do you use probing to generate new ideas and develop new products and services as you encounter unmet needs among consumers, and untapped markets?

11. *Profit Projections.* Have you set up pro-forma statements to project when your product or service will break even, and ultimately turn a profit in the marketplace? What are your indicators of brand success or that you are tracking to meet your sales and profit goals?

12. *Passion.* Upon deeper reflection, do you genuinely enjoy the entrepreneurial lifestyle? Is this a life that brings you fulfillment and allows you to live the life you imagined? Is the entrepreneurial lifestyle consistent with your priorities and values?

5. CREATE DEMAND FOR YOUR BRAND

The **D** in brand stands for **BRAND DEMAND**. Ultimately, brand demand is the reason you decided to "DRIVE" in the first place. In essence, you started your business because you believed you had a product or service that would solve problems for people or organizations in a way that generates profits. Now it is time to close the deal. Creating brand demand requires discipline. Brand demand is more than merely sharing social media posts, memes, and quotes for "likes" and "reposts." In order to consistently convert brand demand into sales, you must rely upon traditional strategies to increase brand demand.

Traditionally, increasing brand demand centers on the question of "how do you convert "contacts" into "contracts" or "cash" depending upon the nature of your business? In answering this question, you must begin with daily, weekly, monthly, quarterly, or annual sales quotas based upon a solid sales strategy that outlines key sub-segments of the market and best strategies for interacting and closing deals with each. Remember that this level of detail is needed because each set of diverse consumers may be drawn to your product or services for different reasons. Listed below are some places you want to consider when thinking through your brand demand plan.

Social media. Social media is a game changer for business owners to be able to engage potential customers that were beyond reach prior to this technological advance. However, I have seen some business owners rely upon social media in ways that have been detrimental to their business. First of all, it is called "social" media, not "business" media, which implies you must do something extra to drive demand for a business within a medium of exchange originally designed for "socializing." In addition, you will need to determine which social media platforms best represent your brand, and how exactly you will engage current and potential customers.

Natural networks. Identify your "natural networks" and devise a plan for being more intentional about engaging individuals. By natural network, I mean the places you go and the people you interact with on a regular basis, without any staged events per se'. For example, if you are a parent, you interact naturally with other parents at your child's school or extracurricular activities. You might attend a place of worship regularly, or belong to a civic, social, or community organization where you might want to consider innovative ways to market your business just based on people you interact with regularly.

Attend events. Identify events to attend for networking purposes. Many think of these events as competition, but there may be ways to cooperate and co-exist with competitors to attract customers. For example, people who purchase CDs, clothes, shoes, and jewelry tend to buy from multiple vendors.

Stage your own or co-sponsor events. Develop a signature event that is marketed by your firm or in collaboration with other business owners. For example, if you sell clothes, you might connect with jewelry makers whose jewelry designs and price points match the consumers you target for your clothing design business. I am constantly asked to share the stage with other women who empower, life coach, and advise individuals to live their best professional and personal life ever. We often find ourselves working extremely well together and leave these events strategizing on how we can continue to support each other.

Media (TV, radio, newspaper, magazine interviews). Determine how you might be a guest on local TV or radio programs to discuss your product or service. In order to maximize your opportunities for media interviews, you need a press kit to include the company's overview, key biographies, fact sheet about key accomplishments, product description, press releases, contact information, client testimonials, and high resolution photos and logos.

Website. Think of your website as the central hub for driving brand demand. Be sure you make it easy for people to quickly assess: (1) who you are; and (2) what you have to offer. In addition, make it easy for website visitors to locate the point of purchase for products and services. You also want to encourage inquiries and use of the "contact us" feature so you can engage with potential customers. Be sure you update your website regularly with new information and remove obsolete material. If you do have a heavy social media presence, be sure to invite website visitors to your social media pages via a link.

Blog. Blogging should be considered only if you enjoy writing and desire to do so on a regular basis. As a blogger, think of yourself as a "thought leader" among diverse stakeholders in your field or industry. If done effectively, blogging can elevate you to being recognized as a market leader or subject matter expert. If you can find a way to be objective in your viewpoint, then you may build a reputation for being a "trusted advisor" over time. You may also want to consult resources for how to profit from blogging should you choose this strategy as a driver of brand demand.

Direct Email Marketing. As you generate brand awareness to attract potential and actual customers, think about a direct e-mail marketing strategy to send out information to individuals who have expressed interest in your brand. Direct e-mail marketing is a way to move the conversation from social media and into a more engaging setting. There are several direct e-mail marketing tools on the market. I suggest you use the free trial for a few before purchasing a full subscription. You may consider setting up your own email correspondence using the blind copy feature on your regular e-mail at no additional cost.

MY "DRIVING" LESSONS LEARNED
IN DEFINING MY BRAND

1. **STORY-TELLING.** I had to learn the art of telling my story. The genius is in perfecting opportunities to weave my personal story into my elevator speech in a way that leads to more engagement about the business.

2. **SATISFYING.** I learned that performing the key tasks associated with building a brand satisfies my soul. I thrive on developing new products or services, creating innovative ways to brand them, and seeking new markets for expansion.

3. **STRATEGIC ALIGNMENT.** In building a cohesive brand platform, I built my four (4) practice areas based on my own gifts, talents, skills, and passion.

4. **STUDY SUCCESS.** I immersed myself into the study of iconic brand developers. Among those that had the most influence on shaping my brand management approach include: Mary Kay Ashe, Berry Gordy, Phil Knight, Phil Jackson, Oprah Winfrey, Tyler Perry, Beyoncé, and Howard Shultz.

5. **SOCIAL MEDIA.** I am a late bloomer when it comes to all things technology. However, I learned to embrace social media as a brand management tool for building brand awareness.

6. **SIMPLE STATEMENTS.** I learned to bridge the gap between social media and traditional brand management in making brand statements within the world of "posts."

7. **STYLE.** I learned that I had to style myself consistent with the overall brand of the firm. In addition to wardrobe, hair, and make up, I incorporated other components of style into my overall personal brand, to include professional speech, body language, tone, and mannerism.

8. **SENSELESS.** I learned to resist other people's need for the brand to make sense to them in the early phases of creativity and innovation.

9. **SILENCE.** I learned to work in silence as I couldn't share innovative brainstorms in the early phases of conceptualization. It is much like not sharing a new pregnancy until after the first trimester.

10. **STANDARDS.** I had to set performance measurements and standards in preparing my team to be brand managers.

"Don't let brand pride be the death of your brand's power and potential to grow."

Dr. Quinn Motivates

Now Let's Go!

CHAPTER 5
HAVE YOU MASTERED BUSINESS MANAGEMENT 101?
You must master the backroom operations.

"Building strong brand management systems will grow the topline. Building strong business management systems will protect the bottom line."

Dr. Quinn Motivates

While this chapter will prove to be the most technical of all the chapters in the book, it is paradoxically the most important planning step you will embark upon before you are ready to invite staff, contractors, and collaborative partners to join you in your entrepreneurial pursuit. The first four (4) chapters of the book focused on clarity about your personal commitment to entrepreneurship and clearly defining your core brand from which to launch. Now it is time to "switch gears" and focus on developing comprehensive business management and operating systems. In this chapter, I provide broad ideas and core elements to help you fully understand the details that must go into the business planning and initial implementation processes. No matter if you are just starting up or have been in business for a few years, it is never too late to develop business, operations, and marketing plans to serve as the foundation from which to analyze, organize, plan, and grow your business. Below is my recommendation for the core components of a business, operations, and marketing plan.

INTRODUCTION
1. Give a detailed description of the business and its goals.
2. Develop a mission and vision statement.
3. Discuss ownership and legal structure.
4. Provide an overview of the core competencies, skills, and past relevant experiences of key personnel who will be owners or partners in the business.
5. Perform an environmental scan to include research political, economic, socio-cultural, technological, environmental, and legal factors impacting your business.
6. Conduct a "SWOT" analysis to identify your business's strengths,

weaknesses, opportunities, and threats.
7. Summarize your firm's competitive advantage(s) within the context of your strengths and opportunities in the marketplace.

PART 1: BUSINESS INFRASTRUCTURE AND GENERAL ADMINISTRATION

1. Incorporation
2. Legal structure
3. Location
4. Insurance
5. Business license
6. Tax ID number
7. Set up electronic payment for staff and contractors
8. Office space allocation or location

PART 2: MARKETING PLAN

1. Identify your marketing objectives: what are you trying to achieve in the marketplace?
2. Develop marketing goals for each objective: what are your numeric measurements for having achieved your objectives?
3. Discuss the product or service you will provide: what are the key features and benefits, logo and symbols, tag lines, etc.?
4. Provide a summary of your marketing research: what do you know about your targeted customers' demographics and buying behavior?
5. Provide details of the size of your market and where you plan to enter and build.
6. Explain your brand management strategy for positioning your brand.
7. Highlight key features of your marketing mix using my expanded model of brand management *(product or service, place, price, promotion, production, packaging, partnerships, project management, people management, probing, profit projections, and passion)*.

PART 3: FINANCIAL MANAGEMENT

1. Develop a cash flow statement and explanation for the first year of operation.
2. Develop a projected profit and loss statement.
3. Develop an income projection.
4. Explain your break-even point and expected time to reach it.
5. Provide a balance sheet that comprises your company's assets and liabilities and net worth.
6. Discuss your plan for an accounting system, including protocols and controls.

PART 4: OPERATIONS PLAN

1. Describe your business infrastructure and general administration plan to manage day-to-day operations.
2. Provide details of your human resources and hiring practices.
3. Highlight your plans for addressing legal and licensing needs as appropriate for your business.
4. Outline major standard policies and procedures for internal controls.

PART 5: SUPPORTING DOCUMENTS *(if planning to submit for external funding)*

1. Include resume's of the owner and key personnel.
2. Secure letters of reference.
3. Provide copies of current/past contracts (history of past performance, individual or company).
4. Provide copies of past/current financial statements.
5. Include credit reports to demonstrate your credit worthiness.
6. Include copies of incorporation documents.
7. Provide documents that will contribute to the lender making a favorable decision.

"DASH" BOARDS

"DAILY ACTIVITIES FOR SEEDTIME AND HARVEST"

Once business, operations, and marketing plans are established, you will need to create what I call business "dash boards" for maximizing your driving experience. A dashboard is defined as a control panel located in front of the driver of a vehicle. Items on the dashboard imply that these are the things that the driver controls and can manipulate to adjust as needed along the journey. I conceptualize "DASH" as the "daily activities" that must be controlled and monitored using the biblical principles of "seedtime and harvest". In essence, as you drive towards your entrepreneurial destination to reap a harvest, you will need to monitor at least seven (7) functional areas using the dashboard analogy as follows:

DR. QUINN'S "DAILY ACTIVITIES FOR SEEDTIME AND HARVEST" AT A GLANCE	
Dashboard 1	Marketing and Sales Systems
Dashboard 2	Finance and Accounting Infrastructure and Monitoring Systems
Dashboard 3	Human Resources Acquisition and Management
Dashboard 4	Standard Operating Protocol and Procedures
Dashboard 5	Strategic Advisors, Allies, and Consultants
Dashboard 6	Continued Growth Planning
Dashboard 7	Personal Contingency Plans and Business Exit Strategies

I use the acronym D.A.S.H: "Daily Activities for Seedtime and Harvest" to remind you that growing a business is much like a farmer that grows crops. Think of the business idea as a seed. That seed must be planted and nurtured in order for it to grow and bear fruit. Also, in keeping with the "drive" analogy, think of these seven (7) functions as being mounted on the dashboard. Just as in a car, you must learn to maneuver the various components on the dashboard primarily while the car is in motion. Finally, don't confuse the dashboard with scoreboards. While you do need quantitative indicators of business success, those are set as part of the business plan and are reviewed during the continued growth planning process.

DASHBOARD 1: MARKETING AND SALES SYSTEMS. A key aspect of being driven as an entrepreneur is you must have a "well-oiled" marketing machine. After developing a detailed marketing and sales plan, the next step is to build a robust brand management system outlined in chapter four (4). Within the brand management model discussed, entrepreneurs must focus on what I call "tactical takedowns." Tactical takedowns are those marketing and sales activities that must be managed and monitored on a daily/weekly/monthly basis within the context of meeting sales goals. Here is a list of 20 tactics for your marketing and sales dash board.

1. *Calculate sales goal.* Based on marketing research, untapped potential, and your firm's capacity, set feasible sales goals.
2. *Calculate cost.* Calculate how much it will cost you to reach the sales you identified in calculating your sales potential.
3. *Contemplate capital needs.* Develop a strategy for obtaining the capital needed to support the sales potential.
4. *Consider your capacity to produce and serve.* Live by the principle of "under promise and over deliver." In the start-up years, determine how much product or service you can deliver under various conditions. Be sure to communicate these constraints and conditions in writing prior to clients making a purchase.
5. *Commission all key stakeholders to take responsibility for marketing and sales.* Establish a culture among employees, sub-contractors, and collaborative partners that it is everyone's responsibility to market the company and sell its products and services.
6. *Classify your potential clients and customers.* Devise a

disciplined way to track progress in terms of: (1) building awareness; (2) creating demand; and (3) closing sales.

7. *Cultivate key accounts and relationships.* Identify legal and ethical, yet innovative strategies for engaging key decision-makers for larger business opportunities.

8. *Codify your customer profiles.* Develop demographic profiles of your ideal customers to help shape how you reach and communicate with them on a regular basis.

9. *Contemplate your communications plan.* Determine what marketing channels and mechanisms maximize opportunities to reach and engage diverse stakeholders, including social media, tradeshows, newsletters, holiday or seasonal contact, and personal touch bases.

10. *Create content that is customer-centered.* Create authentic, thought-provoking printed and visual content aimed at "driving people to buy."

11. *Cultivate your creativity.* Maintain an inner-circle of creative minds that can produce attention-grabbing materials and messages in a timely manner. Sketch or draft models to share with creative minds to help you bring your ideas to fruition.

12. *Coordinate campaigns to fit your consumer markets' needs.* Take advantage of seasonal themes to launch marketing campaigns. For example, as a life coach, I launch major campaigns in December and January when people are naturally thinking about committing to life changes.

13. *Complete your firm's capabilities statement.* For service-driven and consulting firms, develop a high quality publication for emphasizing your expertise, skills, knowledge, and other competitive advantages.

14. *Compile documents needed for a typical proposal.* Review the general anatomy of requests for proposals (RFP) that are typically associated with your industry. To the extent possible compile the various components ahead of time, and when an actual RFP is

issued, you merely have to tweak your pre-written proposal to fit the current request.

15. *Celebrate your customers, employees, and key partners.* Create cost effective ways to celebrate those that support your business, as well as those who helped you build the brand.

16. *Coordinate a calendar of concerted marketing events.* Once you set a marketing strategy in motion, you need to develop a tightly managed calendar of events.

17. *Commit to community service and committee work.* Be visible in the community in which you practice, and among the customers who buy your products.

18. *Conduct competitive analysis.* Keep current and emerging competitors on your radar screen by monitoring their websites, brand proposition, reputation in the market place, current sales and profits, key customers, and competitive advantages.

19. *Close new deals.* Focus on turning brand demand into dollars in the bank. Identify the best methods for reaching your audience and ask for the business. Always remember in sales and marketing that there is no such thing as NO. No means, No, not right now.

20. *Close out underperforming products or services.* Know when a particular brand's season or shelf life is over, and have an appropriate strategy to exit the marketplace.

DASHBOARD 2: FINANCE AND ACCOUNTING INFRASTRUCTURE AND MONITORING SYSTEMS

The second dashboard that must be monitored centers on finance and accounting. Every entrepreneur needs to thoroughly understand the overall financial health of the company. Perhaps the strongest incentive for maintaining strong financial and accounting systems is that it minimizes the likelihood of getting into IRS trouble, or mismanaging funds that could be of criminal magnitude in some cases. Internal controls also limit "theft by taking" of your firm's time, technology, and supplies. Other practical motivation for keeping up-to-date financial statements include: (1) they contribute to making sound business decisions around financial projections; (2) they provide data for "what-if scenarios" related to changes in select variables; and (3) they provide facts for sensitive discussions with managers and staff about budgets and cash flow.

There are four (4) key financial statement formats that every entrepreneur must learn how to read and ultimately use in financial analysis and business decision-making. These statements include: (1) pro-forma statements; (2) profit and loss (P&L) statements (income statement); (3) cash flow statements; and (4) balance sheets (statement of financial position).

Pro Forma Statements. Pro forma statements are for planning purposes to predict how you think the product or service will perform in the marketplace over a certain period of time and what you think it will cost you to get the product or service up and running given start-up expenses, as well as on-going administrative and operations costs. Your projections must be based on industry research and realistic assumptions about what it will cost you and what the returns are on your investments. You want to avoid overstating your potential revenue and understating the expenses associated with your business. You should create pro-formas for every new product or service you develop. This helps you track expenses against revenue as you begin your marketing and sales campaign. Key components of a pro-forma statement include: (1) revenue projections; (2) startup cost; (3) operating costs; (4) variable expenses; and (5) fixed expenses.

Profit and Loss (P&L) Statements (Income Statements). Once you have been in business for at least a year, you should begin to manage your pro-forma statements as actual performance, which is known as a profit and loss or P&L statement. In simple terms, this statement is an official listing of all the sales or revenues in one column and all of the costs or expenses in another. The difference between the total sales and the total cost will either result in a break even, loss, or profit. The core components of the P&L statement are the same as the pro-formas you set up as forecasting. However, now you are using actual and accurate financial data to replace the projected performance for your product or service. It is a good practice to compare the forecast to your actual financial performance. Think critically about what accounts for the deviation in projected vs. actual performance whether it be favorable or negative. Use this analysis to make "data-driven" decisions for your business.

Cash flow statements. A cash flow statement documents the amount of cash that flows in and out of your operation at key periods of time. The cash flow statement shows when cash is expected to be received and when it must be paid out to meet operating obligations, including payroll, recurring bills, and debt service on any business loans you may have. Depending upon the nature of the business, some business owners manage cash flow weekly, monthly, or even quarterly with an annual review for strategic planning purposes. The key question to ask yourself on a consistent basis is "are you making enough cash to meet your business obligations, and eventually turn a profit?"

From a business analysis perspective, cash flow statements document where the company's cash is coming from and where it is going. Cash flows in and out of your business in three broad categories: (1) operating; (2) investing; and (3) and financing. Operating expenses capture the flow of cash for day-to-day operating expenses. Investing activities include such things as major purchases, sales of assets, or loans to others in your supply chain. Financing activities reflect cash flow associated with investments and loan sources. Data from the cash flow statement are used to calculate what is known as a "liquidity ratio", which informs how much cash is on hand or assets that can be quickly converted to cash to settle debts if needed. You can also review cash flow statements to track expenses over time, and to monitor operating and growth projects underway.

Balance Sheet (Statement of Financial Position). A balance sheet is defined as an itemized statement which lists the total assets and the total liabilities of your company, thereby providing a visual of your net worth at a given moment in time. It provides a snapshot of the company's financial health related to assets, liabilities, and equity. It is called a "balance sheet" because "assets" minus "liabilities" must equal the owner's equity. Balance sheets assist in determining if you are using your assets efficiently and managing your liabilities effectively as you drive towards maximizing profit. Assets and liabilities are further divided into current (short-term) and non-current (long-term). There are several components within each sub-division such as cash on hand, inventory, property, accounts payable, and business bank loans. The diverse sub-components depend upon the nature of the business and industry within which you operate.

DASHBOARD 3: HUMAN RESOURCES ACQUISITION AND MANAGEMENT

In this section I provide the fundamental technical portions of human resources management that are typically associated with having individuals classified as "employees". In the next chapter on creating your dream team, I go into details about strategies and options for staffing and teaming. For this dashboard, I focus in on those classified as "employees" in terms of how to manage and monitor your human resources dashboard at key phases as follows:

Phase 1: Pre-hire planning

1. Analyze your human resources needs and options carefully. (See chapter six (6) on the various human resource strategies, including pros and cons, and best practices for unique categories of labor.)
2. Develop relationships with human resources specialists. Determine the extent to which you can barter, pay for essential human resources services, or request online resources to help you build a human resource system that works for your business.
3. Become intimately acquainted with the rules and guidelines on employee classification for legal and tax purposes.
4. Develop comprehensive job descriptions using industry standards and formats for your business. There are some general components that should be included in all job descriptions, such as educational requirements, knowledge, skills, technical competencies, and past

work experiences needed to qualify. You should also include key features of your firm and work environment.

5. Research market-rates for compensation and benefits packages for key personnel.

6. Develop a list of entrepreneurial and growth qualities that all employees must display.

7. Develop an employment handbook of policies and procedures that address the following: statement of mission, goals, values, workday policy, payment policy, performance reviews, promotions and wage increase procedures, employee benefits, leave policy, holiday, vacation, use and ownership of work-related materials, bereavement leave policy, drug and alcohol policy, dress code, disciplinary process, and termination procedures. You should also include statements that policies can change and how employees will be notified of official changes. Other important statements include: (1) explaining that employment is "at will"; (2) clarifying that the employment manual is not a contract; and (3) stating that your firm is an equal opportunity employer.

8. Establish what constitutes "benefits" at your firm. For smaller firms, you may want to point out common benefits that are often taken-for-granted as entitlements in the workplace. For example, if you offer paid vacation, paid holidays, paid personal days, flexible work hours, or time off to attend classes, you may want to document how these benefits are earned and under what conditions they can be used.

9. Build a benefits package that is relevant to your workforce. Many companies are moving towards "customizing benefits" where individual employees select from a "menu of eligible benefits" that fit their lives and obligations, such as medical, mental, dental, and vision plans, retirement pensions, student loan repayment, bonuses, continued educational reimbursement, gym membership, stock options, royalty payments, dependent care, or disability insurance.

Phase 2: Initiating the hiring process

1. Determine how and where you will post your job openings. Enlist the help of colleagues who do similar work to vet resume's and screen applicants.

2. Screen resume's carefully and objectively looking for minimum skills required first. Identify key accomplishments and other items that make the person stand out from the rest. You also want to examine gaps in employment history, patterns of job-hopping, and areas that might render them "difficult to manage" within an entrepreneurial work environment.

3. Interview at least three (3) qualified candidates even if there is an "obvious" front runner. To cut cost and time, initial interviews can be conducted via phone. I suggest conducting the second interview at a neutral location, especially if you have a home office.

4. Make the final hiring decision based on qualifications that fit with your current business environment and your vision for growth. Be clear to hire for current skills, strength, and competencies, and NOT for potential and convenience of availability.

5. Conduct a reference, criminal, character, and financial background check before making an official offer, if possible. If not, state in the offer letter that the final offer is contingent upon the applicant passing a background check.

6. Issue an official offer letter. Under no circumstances are you to imply that the offer constitutes an employment contract. Other key things to put in writing include a starting date, job title, summary of role and responsibilities, compensation, benefits, contingencies that must be addressed prior to start of employment, and the time for responding to the offer.

7. Be prepared for the top-candidate to present a counter offer or even decline the job altogether. As such, do not tell other candidates that a hiring decision has been made until the selected applicant accepts the position. In case your first choice doesn't work out, you want to be able to make an offer to the next person

in line without having to explain that the first person declined so we are offering you the job. In like manner, you might want to prepare a positive closure letter to those who were interviewed and didn't get selected in case you have other positions they may qualify for in the future.

Phase 3: On-boarding new hires

1. Provide each new employee with a comprehensive human resources policy and procedures manual. Be sure to obtain a signature that the new employee has received and reviewed the company's policy handbook.
2. Conduct a formal orientation to review key aspects governing the day-to-day functioning of employees in the workplace.
3. Make formal introductions and arrange for detailed meetings with key staff, clients, and partners that impact the new hire's job.

Phase 4: Managing, maintaining, and developing human resources

1. Adhere to all policies, procedures, taxes, and insurance payments legally required for organizations with employees.
2. Initiate a thorough work plan to manage the first year of job performance.
3. Institutionalize a six (6)-month intense technical skills-building and professional development plan.
4. Encourage self-evaluation and assessments prior to the official performance review.

Phase 5: Transitioning human resources

In coaching new entrepreneurs, many confide in the early years that they are intimidated when it comes to terminating employees. To soften the unfortunate task, I advised them to replace the word "termination" with "transition." I also provide perspectives that as companies grow or experience volatility in the marketplace, human resources needs change. In addition, once promising and suitable employees may experience life-altering changes or shifts in career interests that makes it necessary to transition. In this way, transitioning an employee can take on several forms, and does not always equate to termination on bad terms. First, employees can "transition within" the company. They can "transition up" to take on greater responsibility typically as a promotion. They can "transition laterally" to take on another position that requires a shift in responsibilities. They could "transition down" to a lesser position with or without a pay decrease. While transitioning down theoretically is an option, I strongly recommend avoiding it at all cost. The primary reason is that more times than not, it results in lowered morale, and passive-aggressive approaches to work performance that triggers a need to micro-manage under very negative interactions. It merely serves to prolong the inevitable of "transitioning out."

"Transitioning out" may include several options, such as: (1) helping employees find a more suitable position at another company; (2) assisting them with starting their own firm; or (3) providing support as they transition to school for additional training and education. Depending upon the circumstances and the factors driving the need for transition, you may have to transition someone out with or without cause. Transitioning someone out "with cause" is the toughest transfer of all and may result in emotionally charged retaliations, equipment and documents sabotage, or even legal issues.

As you become more comfortable in your role as "President and CEO", you will develop a "sixth sense" about when it is time to transition employees and under which conditions you should engage diverse individuals in customized transition plans. When transitioning under any type of scenario, be sure you diligently review the work the individual was responsible for over the last six (6) months as many people quit mentally before they leave the job physically.

DASHBOARD 4: STANDARD OPERATING PROTOCOL AND PROCEDURES

Once you begin to hire staff, it is imperative that you institutionalize standard operating protocols (SOP). Without documenting how you want things done, you run the risk of every individual developing her own way of doing things, which could cost time, money, and create chaos and confusion among project team members. Without documented standards, new employees will burden existing staff in trying to learn undocumented protocols and standards of operating.

The list of procedures below is just to get you thinking about the things employees take for granted, and before you know it, have devised their own little personalized system. There may be many more that you will add to your unique office situation even if it is a home office. Establish and publish procedures, as well as reprimands for the following:

1. *General Administration and Daily Office Procedures.* (1) daily office opening and closing procedures; (2) mail pick up and distribution, (3) phone calls during work, including the use of personal cell phones; (4) use of social media and computer for personal use during work hours, (5) non-employee visits to office; (6) décor and allowed personal appliances in the office; (7) office and supply room maintenance; (8) access key cards; (9) office door keys; (10) telephone systems; (11) office furniture inventory, (12) physical office space assignments; and (13) office moves.
2. *Ethical code of conduct.* (1) appropriate use of company property and resources; (2) theft by conversion; (3) theft of time; (4) confidentiality; (5) conflicts of interest; and (6) other conduct that presents as an appearance of impropriety.
3. *Electronic Equipment.* Policies governing use of: (1) computers; (2) tablets; (3) smart phones; (4) cameras; (5) video recorders; (6) copiers; (7) printers; and (8) software. For electronic equipment of value, detail proper procedures to report loss, stolen, or damages to company issued equipped.

4. *Inter-Office Communications.* Establish and publish formal protocols for business communications to include: (1) business and operations memo template and format; (2) ethical guidelines on verbal, written, and electronic communications; (3) a master calendar of events; and (4) a staff meeting general agenda template and format.

5. *Customer service and complaints.* Establish protocols for enhancing customer service, as well as handling customer complaints such as: (1) quality assurance for customer services and customer complaint procedures; and (2) confidentiality in handling client and customer personal information.

6. *Budgeting and accounting.* Institutionalize budgeting and accounting procedures that guard against mismanagement and theft, including: (1) general accounting system and day entry procedures; (2) finance and accounting calendar; (3) disbursement of funds; (4) petty cash management; (5) check requests procedures; (6) project-related inventory purchases; (7) non-budgeted operating and asset purchase requests; and (8) expense report reconciliations.

7. *Employee tracking systems.* Document protocols for: (1) business mileage and travel; (2) time and attendance; (3) payroll tracking; and (4) vendor and sub-contractor management and payment.

8. *Information technology.* Document the rules governing your information technology to include protocols for: (1) securing electronically-stored information; (2) password protections; (3) website updates, (4) company social media posts and comments; (4) personal social media posts and comments; (5) email address utilization; (6) shared drive management; (7) software purchasing and loading; (8) computer virus protection and removal; and (9) external information technology support management (i.e. Go to my pc, constant contact, webhost, survey monkey, etc.)

9. *Annual events.* Create a shared calendar of annual events that may include: (1) annual holiday luncheon/dinners, (2) project management dates; (3) formal business events; (4) performance review period; (5) office cleaning and purging, and (6) inventory of equipment.

10. *Human resources and employment forms.* (1) employee personal data forms; (2) W-4 forms, (3) leave request forms; (4) employee status change form; (5) employee time sheets; (6) employee discipline documentation form; and (7) annual performance review form; (8) employee reference check form; (9) application for employment; (10) employment reference phone script; (11) authorization agreement for direct deposit; (12) emergency contact form; (13) employee incident form; and (14) exit interview questionnaire.

DASHBOARD 5: STRATEGIC ADVISORS, ALLIES, AND CONSULTANTS

In the early years it is unlikely that you will staff seasoned individuals with strategic planning competencies that contribute to growth. Here are some suggestions that could give you access to experienced strategic thinkers:

1. Form or join a CEO mentor group.
2. Form a board of diverse advisors.
3. Join trade associations for your industry.
4. Join professional social media groups.
5. Form or join a think-tank or mastermind group.
6. Reserve some funds for hiring consultants or enter barter agreements with professionals to assist in thinking through complex business problems or specialty area business issues where expert opinions matter.

DASHBOARD 6: CONTINUED GROWTH PLANNING.

Commit to an annual growth planning period. Most entrepreneurs conduct their growth planning in November or December in preparation for the new calendar year. Others who market to the government conduct their growth planning in the summer to be in sync with the government's fiscal year, which begins October 1. No matter your planning period, be sure to build in quarterly meetings to review your progress. As a starting point for continued growth planning, I recommend shaping your continued growth plan around five (5) key components embedded in my "SMART" Growth Model.

DR. QUINN'S "SMART" GROWTH MODEL	
S State of current business	• Analyze revenue, expenses, and profit margins • Review the current state of personnel • Highlight success/failure factors • Conduct a competitive analysis • Identify threat(s) to your business environment • Note any changes in operating costs
M Mission, milestones, and markets	• Revisit your overall mission and vision statements • Document milestones and success measurements • Analyze marketplace dynamics and untapped potential
A Aspiration	• Detail new products or services you aspire to launch
R Risk and Rewards	• Develop a plan to grow sales • Identify changes you need to make to your marketing mix • Document plans to increase profitability
T Talent and Teaming	• Identify human resources needed to reach new growth goals • Identify new partnership and teaming opportunities

DASHBOARD 7: PERSONAL CONTINGENCY PLANS AND BUSINESS EXIT STRATEGY. Every entrepreneur should think through "the end game," which centers on answering the question "Where do you want to be at the end of your pursuit personally and financially? As simple as this question appears to be, most entrepreneurs struggle with answering it. I have provided guidance on how to respond to this question in two distinct ways. First, think self-preservation in terms of a contingency plan for yourself as founder, president, and CEO. Then, turn your attention to diverse strategies for exiting the business.

Founder, president, and CEO contingency planning. Most entrepreneurs are "lifestyle" driven, meaning they set out to start businesses that they whole-heartedly enjoy. Because of the love most entrepreneurs have for the products or services they introduce into the marketplace, they tend to avoid altogether conversations about business exit strategies. To accommodate this intense love affair with one's entrepreneurial enterprise, I attempt to soften the hard conversation of exit strategy through a narrative of "preparing personal contingency plans" as a starting point. In developing your personal contingency plan in a way that maximizes your options out as a business owner, I advise you do the following: (1) prepare and review bi-annually your living will and testimony; (2) invest in health, disability, and liability insurance; (3) establish and contribute regularly to a retirement investment account; and (4) determine the extent to which you benefit from being a W-2 salaried employee or being a 1099 contractor with your own company. The decisions to be made in regards to your personal contingency impact your risks, taxes, and personal income for living expenses and disposable income.

Assessing options for exiting the business. Most entrepreneurs have so much passion and pride for businesses they build from the ground up that they can't even fathom the need to "begin with the end game in mind". There are several factors that can help you grasp which exit strategies might be more appropriate for you. For example if you started your company to change the world, then you will probably be more interested in exit strategies that maintain your involvement in the company. If your motive for starting your own business was that you despised working for someone else, then strategies where you would in fact have a boss may not be as attractive to you. That said, the right exit strategy depends a lot on the owner's objectives. A large part of your decision will depend on whether or not you want to continue to manage your business after you leave it. Prior to selecting a particular exit strategy, consider the following: (1) your long-term liquidity needs; (2) your desire to continue to participate in your company's future growth as a consultant, advisor, or employee working for a new owner; and (3) future marketplace and industry trends for your products or services.

Explore diverse business exit strategies. Here are four (4) exit strategies that are available to most entrepreneurs: (1) bleed the company dry using legal and ethical tactics to pay taxes, investors, employees, partners, and then yourself and simply close the business; (2) sell to friendly buyers such as customers, employees, children, or other family members; (3) sell to non-acquaintance buyers; or (4) pursue an initial public offering (IPO).

Once you immerse yourself in these diverse types of exit strategies, you might determine that a dual approach might be appropriate. For example, if you have distinct departments or brands, then an existing employee might want to invest in a portion of the business that she knows, helped build, and can sustain. Other brands or divisions might be attractive to external investors who see your product or service as filling a gap in their current portfolio. Every exit strategy has its own set of pros and cons. However, in exploring exit options, resolve that no matter how you ultimately leave, it will be done with the utmost of dignity and integrity as your reputation and relationships are just as valuable over the longer run.

MY "DRIVING" LESSONS LEARNED
IN BUILDING BUSINESS AND OPERATIONS SYSTEMS

1. **BUSINESS PLAN.** I wrote my business plan in year two (2) of the business. I now update it annually. It is never too late to write a comprehensive business plan.

2. **BASIC BUSINESS.** In the thick of doing technical work or servicing clients, I allowed basic business administrative tasks to fall through the cracks. I institutionalized what I call "administrative Mondays" where I spend the first four hours doing mundane business chores.

3. **BANKING.** I learned to use small business banking tools to my advantage. I built a relationship with branch managers. I set up systems to assure people got paid on time, taxes were paid quarterly, and that paperwork needed for various business functions were easily retrieved from the online-banking system.

4. **BACKGROUND CHECKS.** I learned to use comprehensive hiring processes that include full reviews of resume's, biographical sketches, and behavioral profiles for best fits.

5. **BARTER.** I keep technical experts on speed dial, but not on payroll. I begin business discussions with options for bartering as a first step in obtaining access to technical experts.

6. **BOUNDARIES AND BOTTOM LINES.** Don't' assume that everyone will take the moral high ground and execute with ethical standards in carrying out their responsibilities and functions. Set firm boundaries and bottom lines and do not allow them to be easily broken or crossed.

7. **BUSINESS 101.** I cross-trained public health staff on business and operations functions based on their strengths and interests.

8. **BRAND MANAGEMENT.** I institutionalized proven brand management techniques for all new products, projects and services.

9. **BRAINSTORM.** I remained flexible in my creativity to solve business problems with scarce resources.

10. **BRICK WALLS AND BLIND SPOTS.** I simply didn't know what I didn't know. I had to learn to recover relatively quickly from running into brick walls and blind spots.

"A business plan puts you in the entrepreneurial game, but executing with excellence keeps you in the game."

Dr. Quinn Motivates

Now Let's Go!

CHAPTER 6

HAVE YOU BUILT A VISION FOR YOUR DREAM TEAM?

You need a core team of courageous followers.

"If you don't take the time to bring the right people on board at the right time under the right conditions, then your dream team will give way to a nightmare."

Dr. Quinn Motivates

As your business grows, you will need to make quick decisions about how to staff important functions. No book per se' can provide a precise formula on how to approach human resources needed to maintain and grow your business. Also understand that no matter your initial teaming plan and process, you will need to revisit your human resources configuration more often than you care to imagine over the life course of your business. In this chapter, I highlight the most commonly used options, and provide my expert opinion on potential advantages and disadvantages, as well as best practices associated with the various options. These options include: (1) bartering; (2) teaming agreements; (3) business partners; (4) independent contractors; (5) employees; (6) interns; and (7) family and friends.

Option 1: Bartering. The first teaming relationship I recommend for new entrepreneurs in particular is that of bartering. Some of the most bartered professional services are legal, human resources, computer technology, marketing, and website design. Bartering allows you to trade services or goods your business needs for the services or goods your business provides. Bartering isn't always a bargain, however, as many of the services and products may not be equivalent in actual cost. Nevertheless, the tradeoff of a non-monetary exchange may be worth giving up some additional hours of service or products.

DREAM TEAM OPTIONS AT A GLANCE: BARTERING	
ADVANTAGES	**DISADVANTAGES**
1. Ideally, there is no monetary exchange, which allows working capital to remain intact 2. Potential access to resources initially deemed unaffordable, i.e. legal, human resources, information technology, marketing, sales, and brand strategy experts	1. Cost of goods and services bartered may not be equitable 2. Barter partners may not be available when needed due to attention on paying clients

BEST PRACTICES IN BARTERING

1. Establish bartering boundaries to safeguard against overextending your services beyond what you can support without monetary exchange.

2. Restrict bartering for services that are deemed "bare essentials" for your business. Avoid bartering for luxury goods or personal perks.

3. Calculate the true value of the products or services you will barter from your business. Know the cost of the products or services you will obtain from bartering with other businesses. Determine if the difference in the cost of products or services offered on either end is worth negotiating for a more equitable exchange.

4. Vet potential barter partners as if money was going to exchange hands.

5. Begin barter agreements with short-term, straight-forward arrangements. Once the relationship is solidified and the value of the barter exchange has been proven to be mutually beneficial over time, then consider longer-term options.

6. Document the barter agreement in writing with all details clearly delineated.

7. Consult with an accountant on recommended methods for recording and reporting barter products and services in ways that comply with IRS laws.

Option 2: Teaming agreements. A teaming agreement is when two independent firms come together for an expressed business objective that has a finite timeline and business deliverables that are clearly delineated. The goal typically centers on leveraging the strengths of the involved entities to collaborate on finding additional revenue streams and new market entry points.

DREAM TEAM OPTIONS AT A GLANCE: TEAMING AGREEMENTS	
ADVANTAGES	**DISADVANTAGES**
1. Opportunity to explore business synergy on a short-term basis prior to committing to a full-fledged business partnership 2. Leverage others' products and/or services as strategic advantages in pursuing bigger market share 3. Teaming partners typically understand they will not be compensated for writing proposals and pitching presentations collectively to win new work 4. Teaming agreements typically are based on strengths and areas of expertise for all partners	1. Sharing information about your clients, partners, network, products, and services with a potential competitor 2. Short term agreements must be revisited after each venture is completed which eats into execution and creative time 3. Time-consuming to vet teaming partners and build relationships 4. Easy to deviate from the spirit of the agreement as it is difficult to monitor and enforce "work ethics" and "hustle"

BEST PRACTICES IN TEAMING AGREEMENTS

1. Develop a "Memorandum of Understanding (MOU)" or "Teaming Agreement" detailing how members of the team will: (1) generate leads; (2) pitch as a team for business; (3) distribute workloads; (4) be compensated; (5) and include the terms for extending the teaming agreement.
2. Teaming agreements should specify start and end dates, terms and conditions for extending and ending the agreement, and what constitutes project or service completion.
3. Maintain a business approach to teaming by conducting a "SWOT" analysis which is an acronym for identifying your company's (a)

strengths, (b) weaknesses, (c) opportunities, and (d) threats. Use the findings as guidance on what teaming options would put you in the best position to meet your business goals.

4. Vet individuals from "friends and family" networks using the same processes you would to vet unknown business owners in the teaming process. Inquire about their past teaming collaborations.
5. Initiate candid discussions about business culture, values, and ethics.
6. Determine how all entities will contribute working capital (financial or sweat equity) to the partnering activities and programs.
7. Institutionalize team touch-bases as the norm. This alleviates beginning difficult conversations when there is tension or a crisis brewing.

Option 3: Business Partners. A business partnership is a legally binding agreement between two or more individuals. The catch phrase is "legally binding." Most people neglect to hammer out the details of the partnership and legally obligate the partnership via a signed agreement. In fact, I am often called in to rescue joint business ventures launched between two friends or relatives on sheer excitement and enthusiasm. What I discover is that most individuals are trustworthy and possess good character and integrity. However, they simply didn't plan for blind spots and external environmental situations that erode trust and agitate business deals sealed with firm handshakes.

Should you pursue a business partnership, understand that you are embarking upon a long-term relationship that will need to be nurtured, strengthened, and cultivated with patience and trust. In essence, if you are not already married to this person, be prepared to treat him or her like a work spouse. As you consider what technical expertise you gain through a business partnership, think through issues such as: (1) Can you stand to be around and work with this person 24/7?; (2) How will you solve conflicts?; (3) Will it be 50/50 investments, or will working capital and sweat equity be split in some other fashion?; (4) Is this your real life spouse and if so, is the marriage strong enough to withstand the additional pressures of working together?; (5) Do you get along with each other's families and friends?; (6) Can you both set and abide by personal and professional boundaries that cannot necessarily be enforced by a contractual agreement?; and (7) Are you willing and capable of carrying the financial and/or work load if your business partner has personal issues that take them away from the entrepreneurial pursuit for some period of time?

DREAM TEAM OPTIONS AT A GLANCE: BUSINESS PARTNERS	
ADVANTAGES	DISADVANTAGES
1. Mutual support and motivation as business partners tend to share kindred entrepreneurial spirits of "all in" 2. Shared cost of start-up 3. Shared responsibilities and work 4. Shared business risks and expenses 5. Ideally, partners' skills, resources, networks, and expertise are complementary	1. The partnership takes on the persona of a marriage 2. Partners bringing less to the table may be relegated to "staff-like" treatment, especially when it comes to strategic business decisions 3. In general partnership agreements, all partners are jointly and individually liable for the business activities of the other, meaning if your partner skips town, you are liable for all business debts incurred 4. The slightest differences of opinion and disagreements could ignite personal and professional tensions, rifts, or even "irreconcilable differences" 5. Bankruptcy of a partner or the partnership impacts all entities involved 6. A partner can withdraw voluntarily or involuntarily 7. Capital distribution can become complex in terms of financial capital vs. sweat equity

BEST PRACTICES IN BUSINESS PARTNERSHIPS

1. Conduct an executive session with yourself to honestly assess whether or not you can thrive in a partnership arrangement. Think long and hard about your ability and willingness to share space, ideas, decision-making, and future goals.

2. Decide upon your criteria, values, standards, and deal-breakers in selecting a business partner. Think about the extent to which you and any potential partner have the same motivation, values, work habits, and ethics, vision, ideas, and business objectives. In addition, understand how your skills and strengths complement each other.

3. Consider a short-term teaming agreement option as a "courting period" before entering a longer term business partnership.

4. Initiate frank, upfront, candid, open, transparent discussions to achieve absolute clarity from the beginning as it relates to "agendas," including business, personal, shared, and hidden.

5. Even if you are going into business with a spouse, friend, or family member I highly recommend that you plan and structure the business partnership as if all entities were personal strangers.

6. Do not enter a business partnership with anyone living pay check to pay check or who have not made provisions to take the risks needed to pursue entrepreneurship.

7. Determine the legal structure of the partnership (general partnership, limited partnership, or a limited liability partnership).

8. Develop and sign an iron-clad partnership agreement that includes, at a minimum, your shared understanding of the following: (1) management; (2) profit and loss distribution; (3) voting powers and methods; (4) withdrawal from or dissolution of the partnership; (5) percentage split of ownership; (6) job titles and descriptions, (7) salary payments, and (8) responsibility for company debts and liabilities.

9. If you can afford it, I suggest consulting a lawyer and an accountant to help form your partnership and to draw up the legal agreements.

10. Once an agreement is entered into, put all co-decisions made thereafter in writing and sign and date.
11. You can only document and sign so much in a formal agreement. Therefore you must do a "gut check." By gut check I mean asking yourself, "In my heart of hearts and deep within my guts, do I wholeheartedly trust this person?"

Option 4: Independent contractor. An independent contractor (IC) is a person or business that provides goods or services to another organization under terms and conditions documented in a written or verbal agreement. ICs set their own schedules, generally, and are governed by deliverables. You lose some control over how tasks are performed, which could impact quality and standards you have set for your brand. ICs may have additional projects and may have less commitment than an employee.

INDEPENDENT CONTRACTORS	
ADVANTAGES	DISADVANTAGES
1. In the absolute, you will save money by reducing employee-related overhead expenses (payroll, taxes, benefits, insurances, etc.) 2. In general, ICs require less management, monitoring, and motivation 3. ICs are responsible for their own permits, professional licenses, and continuing their own professional education 4. Provides optimum staffing flexibility as you can match qualified independent contractors with tasks and projects as work becomes available	1. Misclassifying ICs can result in financial penalties from your state or the IRS, including liabilities for employment tax, and interest 2. Your right to terminate an IC's services is limited by the terms of your written IC agreement 3. ICs are not covered by workers' compensation, which means that you are at risk for being sued for job-site injuries 4. They will promote their own brand and company 5. Higher probability of getting audited by IRS when you use too many ICs 6. Lack of control over ICs' time and project management.

BEST PRACTICES IN HIRING INDEPENDENT CONTRACTORS

1. Review and abide by all local, state, and federal guidelines classifying a person as an independent contractor.

2. Be sure your independent contractor agreements includes: (1) a description of the services to be performed; (2) fee for services, terms and conditions for payment; (3) start and end dates; (4) key deliverables; (5) an explanation of who will be responsible for expenses, materials, equipment, and office space; (6) a statement that you and the worker agree to an independent contractor relationship; (7) a statement that the contractor has permits and licenses the state requires to do the work; (8) a statement that the contractor is responsible for paying state and federal income taxes; (9) an acknowledgment by the IC that he or she is not entitled to any of the benefits you provide employees; (10) a statement by the IC that he or she carries liability insurance; (11) a description of the circumstances under which you or the IC can terminate the agreement, and, (12) an explanation of how you and the IC will resolve any disputes.

3. Identify who will be responsible for managing contractual deliverables and signing off on invoices and under what conditions will work be considered complete.

4. Make arrangements to own all copyrights if the work is indeed your intellectual property. Share copyrights as appropriate with independent contractors who contributed to book chapters, documentaries, etc.

Option 5: Employees. An employee is defined as a person employed by your company for a wage or salary. When you get to the point of hiring employees, you must apply legal, fair labor practices, and comprehensive hiring processes to onboard employees. To legally acquire employees requires rigorous over-sight, including recruiting, hiring, managing, monitoring, measuring, developing, and motivating employees. On average, employee-related expenses add 40 percent to your overall payroll costs. For example, if you pay an employee $20 per hour, you must pay an additional $8 in required employee expenses, insurance, and taxes. This doesn't include health benefits and retirement contributions. In addition to the costs of payroll processing, the most common employee expenses include: (1) federal payroll taxes; (2) unemployment compensation insurance; (3) workers' compensation insurance; (4) office space and equipment; and (5) employee benefits like paid vacation and health insurance.

EMPLOYEES	
ADVANTAGES	**DISADVANTAGES**
1. Employees have the potential to develop into competent courageous followers and leaders 2. Hiring employees can facilitate business growth 3. Allows you to specify the work schedule of the person you hire, which helps ensure the employee will be available to handle business tasks when you need them performed 4. Allows you to train your employee using strategies best suited for your growth plan 5. Employees typically have pride in their position and may go the extra mile in exchange for appropriate levels of job security	1. In addition to actual salaries, additional payroll costs for employees will range between 20% to 30%, depending upon other factors such as benefits, taxes, and insurance 2. Employees must be accommodated in terms of the resources and work space needed to carry out business tasks 3. Must factor in additional administrative and supervisory, evaluation, and coaching time for each employee 4. Employees can sue for wrongful termination even in a "right to work" state 5. Employer assumes increased liability for all damages, accidents, and mistakes made by each employee performing duties consistent with her job description

BEST PRACTICES IN HIRING EMPLOYEES

1. Conduct a thorough analysis of your needs and capacity for hiring employees by thinking through some key factors governing employee-employer relations, including but not limited to right to control supervision, skill-level, timing and methods of payment, long-term opportunities, and workplace environment and equipment.

2. Establish working capital to support a position for at least two (2) years via savings, credit cards with high limits and low interest rates, or lines of credit.
3. Provide some benefits most commonly associated with a full-time job, such as paid holidays and vacation time, as well as health benefits if funds permit.
4. Maintain cash on hand to meet payroll for employees.
5. Allow for additional administrative hours to oversee payroll paperwork that is legally required.
6. Make arrangements to have funds to pay employees' taxes, social security, Medicare, and unemployment insurance to avoid large tax bills and penalties.
7. Develop a plan for training and developing employees to grow their skills and expertise consistent with the company's growth plan.
8. Purchase general liability insurance.
9. Purchase workers' compensation insurance.
10. Rent, lease, or purchase office space and equipment.
11. Learn and abide by the Affordable Care Act that requires all employers with the equivalent of more than 100 full-time employees (50 in 2016 and later) provide them with minimally adequate health insurance or pay a penalty to the IRS.
12. Learn and abide by labour and anti-discrimination laws at the local, state, and federal levels of governance.

Option 6: Interns. An intern is defined as a student or trainee who works to gain experience in a professional field. Federal regulations require internships at for-profit organizations to be paid, unless the position meets the stringent criteria of a trainee position. There are other employment laws governing the use of interns as a form of cheap labor as it may displace employees who qualify for those jobs. That said, you must create a learning experience, work around the school and extra-curricular activities schedule, and budget for some level of compensation. You can also work collaboratively with schools to provide course credits as a benefit.

Typically interns' expectations are extremely high in terms of what they should be exposed to in the workforce. As such, they are often unmotivated to complete "menial" and "mundane" work assignments. To mitigate this situation and manage expectations, integrate menial tasks into informative learning experiences related to their career choice.

INTERNS	
ADVANTAGES	**DISADVANTAGES**
1. Interns are eager to learn and want to do a great job 2. A graduate intern provides an extra set of capable, educated hands 3. Employers are not obligated to hire interns on a full time basis. 4. Most collegiate students are computer and technologically-savvy 5. Interns are an inexpensive, yet not cheap source of labor.	1. Interns expect access to the owner and are less sensitive to rules governing chain of command 2. Managing work-school-personal life balance is a challenge for collegiate students 3. Interns can take up a lot of time in for mentoring and training 4. Most interns want summer internships, which may not coincide with your company's peak season

BEST PRACTICES IN HIRING INTERNS

1. Avoid prematurely promising a permanent job beyond the internship. Instead, wait until the very end of the internship to make decisions about future employment with your firm.
2. Pre-determine how interns will be supervised by a skilled employee or contractor.
3. Develop a structured work plan for an enriching and mutually beneficial internship experience. The work plan should include manageable, supervised tasks that are tied to the firms' overall goals and objectives.
4. Consider hosting interns for nine (9) to 12 months. Longer internships allow interns to experience the business cycle over key phases. Also, employees get better returns on investments in training, equipment, and time invested in interns.

5. Research partnering with a college or university to become a practicum site for skill-building where you work more intensely with professors and collegiate career placement personnel to align projects with a student's relevant major course work.
6. Consider hosting a cohort of interns as a learning community. This scenario creates healthy peer support and appropriate competition in the workplace.

Option 7: Friends and family. If you notice, I put family and friends last for a number of reasons. Yes, I am sending a symbolic message to make this your very last option for meeting your human resources needs. The primary reason is that if things go wrong, you must face the negative extreme that the business environment can result in rifts in family ties and friendships that cannot be repaired in some instances. If you must employ family or friends, do so for targeted tasks they are qualified to perform. Put them under short-term contracts with signed agreements about their level of compensation or benefits they will reap in exchange for the labor power. Also be careful of referrals from family and friends to hire other individuals. Simply stated, avoid any hiring opportunities to fill seats in a hurry. Additionally, if your company bids for, and is awarded a government contract, family and friends come under a different kind of scrutiny.

| **FAMILY AND FRIENDS** ||
ADVANTAGES	**DISADVANTAGES**
1. Working with family members and friends you like can really be fun and break the isolation in the entrepreneur world	1. Issues of nepotism may surface should non-relative employees raise concern about preferential treatment
2. Real friends and family will pitch in for free in the formative years, and even at a discount rate as you build the business	2. Disgruntled friends and family members tend to vent to other friends and family members
3. Close friends and family typically are willingness to sacrifice for the business	3. Many walk away believing you wronged or used them to build your business
	4. Family tensions and conflicts tend to

FAMILY AND FRIENDS	
ADVANTAGES	DISADVANTAGES
	spill-over into the workplace
	5. Compensation and corrective performance conversations can be awkward
	6. You may get calls from "concerned" family and mutual friends related to your treatment of a particular family member
	7. Friends and family may intentionally or unintentionally undermine your leadership with other employees by not taking you or the rules governing the employment agreement seriously

BEST PRACTICES IN HIRING FAMILY AND FRIENDS

1. Be sure all family and friends have the skill-set and work experiences needed for the position.
2. Do not waive background, reference, and resume' checks if that is your policy for other employees.
3. Manage family and friends in ways that are consistent with your policy for all employees.

BUILDING THE "DREAM TEAM"

The great paradox of building a dream team is that it can become your worst nightmare if you don't manage, grow, and let go of your dream team members at the appropriate times. No matter your initial team configuration, you should be ready to address the need to change team members multiple times. Rapid turnover is the norm in start-ups and your workforce doesn't begin to stabilize until after 10 years of operation. In fact, expect most employees to leave within 18 months if your firm is under 10-years old. In addition, you must develop a thick skin to transition employees in accordance with your policy when people just aren't working out. That said, be really grateful if you can retain an excellent employee for three (3) or more years in your first decade in business. The bottom line is rapid changes, growth, and instability ultimately burnout employees. Even after doing due diligence as detailed in the human resources dashboard in chapter five (5), there is still no guarantee that qualified individuals will mesh together as a high performing team. To help busy entrepreneurs build teams within the context of an already heavy business agenda, I developed the "TEAM" model. The TEAM Model is comprised of 25 concepts that entrepreneurs can apply in building highly effective teams. The concepts collectively address subjective and objective measures in assuring teams are maximizing their performance. As you review these, think of the entrepreneur as a coach prepping a team that has a shot at winning a championship.

25 CORE ELEMENTS OF TEAM-BUILDING

THE "T" IN TEAM

1. *Talent.* There is no substitute for assessing each team member's "raw talent" and growth potential. Talented employees are those that have the right mix of technical competencies, soft skills, and passion for the position or project. In essence, not only are they good at what they do, they tend to thoroughly enjoy the job. Moreover, talented individuals have a certain confidence in their abilities and know how to draw upon their experiences, capabilities, resources, and networks to get the job done under diverse operating conditions.

2. *Typology.* Once talented team players are in place, you want to assess for special skills. This allows you to know who your "go to" team

members are to accomplish certain tasks or projects, particularly under pressure. I recommend the following typology to help you identify how to best position your players on the field: (1) innovators; (2) finishers; (3) analyzers; (4) implementers; and (5) switch-hitters.

   a. **THE INNOVATORS.** Innovators constantly offer fresh ideas and concepts. Not only are they good for helping to develop new models, and shifting paradigms, but they also have a unique way of looking at old or lingering problems with fresh eyes. They have great imaginations and can be a great asset in new business development.

   b. **THE FINISHERS.** Once a new creative idea has been identified and accepted for further development, you need to get your finishers involved. Finishers know how to manage projects for results. They get people committed to play their role, and they utilize resources efficiently and effectively. With some additional leadership development, finishers become great directors and vice presidents.

   c. **THE ANALYZERS.** Analyzers are your in-house critics and quality control experts. They catch all the mistakes and imperfections. They point out all the flaws and see things as black and white, and right and wrong. They revise and correct other employees' work extremely well. If you can stomach their complaints and their personal satisfaction derived from "stomping the boss" then you will do well with this group. I call them secret weapons, who reflect upon and refine the big ideas to perfection. They focus on the facts, flaws, and failures; however, they need the right environment to take the next step of actually "fixing" an issue they analyze.

   d. **THE IMPLEMENTERS.** These are your process worker-bees. Sometimes your analyzers might over-analyze, but the implementers will rally the team around a theme of "just do your job!" They are the realists on the team who understand that you must execute and deliver under imperfect conditions. The implementers are close to the details and the bottom line.

Implementers tend to work extremely well when managed by finishers. While they are excellent at performing a routine task, they may not be the most thorough multi-tasker. However, over time, implementers become valuable resources as they are "by the books" types, and will passively alert authority when others are not in compliance.

   e. **THE SWITCH-HITTERS.** A switch-hitter is defined as one who can play all positions on the team relatively well. Not only do they come to the team as multi-talented individuals, but they love the challenge of learning something new so as to enhance their ability to contribute to the team. They tend to be gifted at project and people management in ways that might earn them the nickname of being a "mini-me" in relations to you as the business owner. Other key characteristics of switch-hitters include flexible, thick-skinned, quick studies, and excellent at multi-tasking.

3. *Talk.* High performing teams talk. They talk to you. They talk to each other. They talk around the water cooler; and they talk about you, the entrepreneur. Because they talk about you, it is your job to give them something positive to talk about, or at a minimum, re-direct misinformation or negative narratives. This requires intentional efforts to communicate with the rank and file using diverse methods, such as formal staff meetings, memos, and informal touch bases.

4. *Trust.* Trust is vital to team building. Trust has emotional (gut feeling) and logical (based on experience) components. For an entrepreneur, building trust is a non-negotiable investment. Because your time is so valuable and your resources are limited, consider bypassing the traditional corporate models for team-building activities that cost money and time out of the office. Instead, use real work projects to integrate team-building opportunities into the natural flow of production. As you observe your team in action, pay close attention to untapped potential and strengths that are being under-utilized. The main thing to remember is that you not only want your team to trust you, but they also must learn to trust each other.

5. *Truth.* You will learn that truth has a subjective and objective reality. Subjective truth is built on "social facts" typically shared through informal conversations and accepted as truth without question. Objective truth is that which is proven and validated with "scientific facts." What happens in most work environments is self-serving versions of the truth often "sliced and slanted" through omission or exaggeration. You must put in work to create a culture of truth derived from faithfulness and honesty. For example, model honesty and "above board" behavior in your own business activities as your employees are observing your every move.

6. *Transparency.* Transparency is operating in such a way that it is easy for others to see what actions are underway in moving the business to the next level. Transparency centers upon openness, constant communication, and accountability. Key components of transparency include disclosing any hidden agendas, owning and disclosing mistakes, and clarity.

7. *Transactional.* Every organization goes through phases where transactional instructions and commands must be followed with precision. I call this the "all-management" aspects of business where the emphasis is on getting the job done. Activities deemed as "transactional" in entrepreneurship include those tasks that are completed within a relatively short-term time frame. Transactional tasks typically require managerial monitoring (as opposed to leadership). In completing transactional tasks, rally the team around meeting finite deadlines with the appropriate short-term rewards and punishments. Transactional managers are needed to institutionalize teaming tasks that are routine, mundane, and require attention to details. Once you have effective transactional managers in place, it frees you as the entrepreneurial leader to work on transformational activities.

8. *Transformational.* Transforming teams is crucial to the strategic development of a small business. As the leader of your entrepreneurial enterprises you must build a team that is ready for the next level of execution. It is your responsibility to press the team towards the future

by introducing change into the system without compromising morale, productivity, and high performance. In fact, transformation strategies work best when they include opportunities for employees to grow personally and professionally as the company evolves.

9. *Tough.* In order to sustain through change or crisis, teams must have a reputation for being tough. Tough teams are characterized as having members with "thick skin" to endure criticism, attacks, and sacrificing self-motives and interests for the team. During tough times, teams need high degrees of loyalty and commitment to remain productive in the midst of chaos, confusion, and external threats. This degree of loyalty and commitment is enhanced when you engage employees to stave off gossip, rumors, and low morale as culprits of trust and productivity. As you navigate tough times, provide employees with an authentic context of the bigger vision, the progress of change, the impact and consequences of a crisis, as well as tentative timelines and a range of possible options to prepare the team for the best and worse-case scenarios. Finally, show you care about them and their overall well-being during tough times by taking a genuine interest in what they are feeling and how they are coping.

10. *Trouble-shooting tools and tactics.* Teams get into "trouble". Trouble is different from tough times in that the latter is driven by: (1) external threats beyond the direct control of the organization or (2) by the entrepreneur's proactive decision to pursue some aggressive growth goal. However, trouble in this context refers to issues emerging from inside the system typically stemming from inner-team conflict, tension, poor judgment, ethical or integrity issues, lack of performance, or inexperience in problem solving. Teams also have "troublemakers" who sabotage relationships, projects, and the overall business strategy. In these instances, avoid allowing your troublemakers to eat up your time with your talented problem-solvers. Remove panic from your system by focusing on clear deliverables and timelines for addressing trouble. Finally, deal justly, legally, and fairly with the root cause of the trouble.

THE "E" IN TEAM

11. *Excellent work.* Instill in your team that excellence is not perfection, but rather it is best practices in motion. Institutionalize excellence via constant feedback and systems improvement. Be sure to plan time for debriefing after major projects, events and campaigns. At the individual level, provide mid-course corrections and feedback prior to the annual assessment process. In addition to excellence in technical work, focus on creating a culture of top-notch professional development. This includes work habits, such as arriving on time and not being in a hurry to rush out of meetings. Excellent work also includes following laws, rules, regulations, protocols and procedures that everyone must comply with no matter one's title, position, pay, or longevity with the company.

12. *Environmentally appropriate.* Teams must be assessed for "fit" in a particular operating and cultural environment beyond having the technical competencies and potential for growth. A desire for environmental appropriateness should not be used to exclude diverse employees. The goal of assessing for "fit" is to maintain a team that has a general spirit of harmony, flexibility, adaptability, and cooperation as they accomplish shared goals. In addition, you want to be sure team members can act as good corporate citizens over the resources, rules, and regulations governing the work environment.

    For entrepreneurs building an inner-circle of courageous followers, as you observe your team in action, ask yourself: (1) "Is this someone I trust with portions of my business"; (2) "Would I want to be trapped in an office with this particular person for three straight days working on a deadline"; and (3) "Do I genuinely like working with this person?" While you would never discriminate against employees who don't pass your "inner-circle test" in terms of promotions and assignments, you have a right to only invite those you trust and are comfortable around into your sacred, more vulnerable space of operation.

13. *Engagement.* Engaged team members feel valued and typically have more energy and enthusiasm to go the distance. As a business owner, you will need to carve out time to engage your team. Engagement is

different from micro-management as engagement centers on developing participatory strategies that enhance cooperation, innovation, creativity, productivity and quality. Micro-management is thought to refer to activities that are controlling, highly reactive, and laced with distrust and lack of confidence in team members' ability to produce high quality results. Engagement strategies include getting team-members' input on problem-solving, suggestions on the root cause of issues, and including them in growth and strategic planning processes.

14. *Empowerment.* Authentic entrepreneurs should focus on creating a culture of empowerment where all are held appropriately responsible for delivering results, and taking responsibility for mistakes, missteps, and failures. An empowered culture is one in which information, resources, power, and authority are shared to a certain degree so that key stakeholders take initiative, make informed decisions, and proactively solve problems. In order to have an empowered environment, you must begin with team members who are competent, skilled, and savvy in how they utilize resources, take calculated risks, and take initiative.

15. *Effective functioning as a family.* Just as with one's family of origin, some aspect of the work environment should signify that members care about each other's health and well-being. Begin with identifying and building upon shared values and interests that cut across positions, titles and job functions. In addition, team members need a certain level of protection and provision regardless of employee position or performance. For example, everyone wants support during time of bereavement of a close family member, or praise and acknowledgement when one of their children achieves a milestone. Entrepreneurs need to create an environment where individual team members look forward to certain rituals that make the work environment fun and secure.

16. *Effective functioning as a business.* Although most small businesses pride themselves on functioning as a "family", ultimately you must engage your team in systems designed to ensure the business functions

effectively. Remind team members that the key to the company's long-term survival is that everyone must respect and abide by the systems governing the business. During conversations with team members, be sure you integrate discussions about human resources, information technology, finance, payroll, marketing and sales, legal, and operating standards and procedures. Intentionally highlight how team members must be effective and efficient in managing resources allocated to them to achieve business results for which they are being held accountable. You might want to overly emphasize budgets and budget management as it impacts the bottom line to guard against wastefulness by team members. Finally, you want to lead teams in activities to help them explore untapped talent, skills, potential, and interest directly related to key business functions. For example, if you run an information technology company, and discover that one of your technicians has a natural charismatic personality that is appealing to clients, then you might want to provide opportunities for her to skill-build in marketing and sales.

THE "A" IN TEAM

17. *Accountability.* All team members must be held accountable for driving towards results. To optimize accountability, teach your team to balance the need to "do the right things" (effective) and to "do things right" (efficient). Also provide guidance on the consequences for not taking responsibility. As some teams can provide too much variation in time, quantity, and quality of work, I caution you to monitor teams for "productivity" vs. "activity." What I have discovered over time is that you cannot "demand" accountability, nor can you "pep talk" accountability into existence. The only way to hold teams fully accountable is you have to "drive" for results. Driving for results include appropriate monitoring and engagement, as well as providing clarity on the company's vision and future.

18. *Aptitude.* Teams need competent members with specialty knowledge in order to remain competitive over the long-term. Aptitude can be acquired or based on natural ability, however avoid confusing "potential" with "actual" performance. Also recognize the tension and conflict that arise when individuals express interest in growth and development and a desire for increased responsibility based on their perceived aptitude. Use the formula of: (1) skills; (2) competences; (3) knowledge, (4) actual past performance; and (5) potential for growth to measure aptitude more objectively. Furthermore, be conscious of the fact that most will want additional pay when performing duties that benefit the company even if they are learning and growing via "on-the-job training". Be clear up front in your policies governing how individuals will be rewarded for acquiring new skills and competencies as part of your firm's growth strategy.

19. *Attitude.* In order to survive, teams must perform, and over time gain a reputation for having a proven track record of getting results. At the same time, team members need positive dispositions and pleasant attitudes in general. A pleasant disposition is characterized as knowing how to respectfully dissent or disagree with decisions being made. Spirits of cooperation should not be confused or substituted for "group consensus" or "group think" as conflict avoidance during decision-making.

20. *Active listening.* Teams need leaders and members who value active listening. How well you listen has a major impact on your firm's overall effectiveness. The quality of your relationships with key contributors is demonstrated by your willingness to listen to them. Active listening serves as a model for showing respect and understanding, however it is not the same as actually agreeing with what you are hearing. You simply are seeking to gain information and perspective. Key characteristics of active listening include: (1) giving the speaker your undivided attention; (2) acknowledging key messages being communicated; (3) looking directly at the speaker; (4) putting aside distracting thoughts; (5) avoiding mental preparation for the rebuttal;

(6) using body language that signals you are paying attention; and (7) allowing the speaker to finish each point uninterrupted.

21. *Agendas.* Agendas should reflect "mutuality of purpose." You should assess business associates for personal and professional agendas by observing and inquiring: (1) why is this person here?; (2) what do they want?; and (3) how can I help them achieve their objectives? Often times, agendas can be discussed during normal communications to share business objectives. However, the more difficult agenda to detect and address is referred to as the "hidden" agenda. As an entrepreneur you must be more vigilant to discover hidden agendas, which typically manifest as dysfunctional behaviors that are inconsistent with the culture of a high performing team, as well as in conflict with what the person verbally expressed as their goals and objectives. One way to be sure "agendas" are aligned, is to integrate discussions about mission, vision, and business objectives into meeting agendas as a way to convey that tactical decisions must align with the overall mission.

THE "M" IN TEAM

22. *Mission-centered.* High performing teams are mission-centered. Everyone on the team must understand the overall mission of the organization and how various jobs contribute to the mission. As the leader of your enterprise, I suggest you develop a clear and concise mission statement. Key questions that should be answered in crafting your mission statement include: (1) what exactly does your company do?; (2) how does the company do it?; (3) who is the company doing it for?; and (4) what value does your products and services bring to the customer? Over time, devise strategies for institutionalizing your mission statement as a framework for working together.

23. *Methods-driven.* Once there is clarity on the team's mission, then members must be engaged in a set of methods aimed at achieving the mission. Business methods are a set of logically related tasks performed to achieve a defined valuable business outcome. Methods are not the enemies of innovation and creativity. In fact, identifying and

documenting rigorous methods actually enhances team cooperation, morale, and fosters cross-functional support as others come to appreciate and anticipate methods (processes) that come before and after tasks they are directly responsible for performing. In addition, you want the team to be clear on what processes generate income, and which ones cost the company money and time.

24. *Motivation.* Motivating teams must address intrinsic and extrinsic factors. When it comes to sustaining motivation, you must find a compelling "WHY"! When engaging individuals in goal setting, they tend to focus on their "I" story. Your role is to redirect them to their "WHY" narrative. The strength of collective "WHYs" among diverse team members is phenomenal in action. At the other extreme, weak "WHYs" typically are supported by excuses and explanations that limit goal pursuit. In order to put motivation into practice, rally your team around four (4) questions for guidance: (1) why do we exist?; (2) what are we supposed to accomplish together?; (3) what are our strategies for achieving our collective goal?; and (4) what tasks must we undertake to assure that we continue to exist?

25. *Moving managers to leaders*. As you assess various team players, you want to look for who is ready to move from being managers to leaders. You are not looking for popular employees, but rather those that have proven to be franchise players. Innovators, finishers, and switch-hitters all have some leadership potential and strengths. For those selected for leadership development, the first order of business is to shift their paradigm on the fundamental differences between leadership and management.

No matter the industry, product, or service, there are some universal leadership competencies that should be displayed before you consider elevating someone to a leadership position, including their ability to: (1) conceptualize innovative approaches for problem-solving and building business; (2) analyze and interpret data for decision-making; (3) lead and decide with limited guidance and information; (4) adapt and cope when initial plans and strategies shift; (5) support and cooperate during tough times; (6) perform and excel with scarce resources, and (7) organize and execute using balanced approaches of transactional and transformational leadership.

Once assessed for growth potential and capacity, invest time in developing leadership skills among promising managers. Coaching individuals from management to leadership entails engaging them in a thorough understanding of the broader business functions and systems, including: (1) human resources; (2) administrative and operations; (3) finance and accounting, and (4) marketing and sales. Moreover, individuals must be given opportunities to master tools and techniques related to business strategy and decision-making to think beyond that which they have managed, and become more of a visionary in leading a brand, project, department, or business development initiative. As with any growing company, it could be tempting to promote good managers into leadership roles. Should you grow at a rate greater than that of your managers' potential to lead, I advise you to hire leaders externally rather than prematurely promote from within. However, you may face another challenge when hiring and promoting from the outside as you run the risk of alienating some dedicated employees and affecting morale adversely.

MY "DRIVING" LESSONS LEARNED
IN BUILDING MY DREAM TEAM

1. **EFFECTIVE CONSULTANTS.** I taught my staff and sub-contractors what it meant to be a consultant and how it differed from being a regular employee. Stay tuned for another book on "52 Characteristics and Attributes of an Effective Consultant"!

2. **EFFICIENT.** I learned to think of time in multiple dimensions for maximizing efficiencies: (1) my personal and social time; (2) my professional time as President and CEO primarily dedicated to new business development and client engagement; (3) my time as a technical contributor to projects; and (4) my time to manage, monitor, and development staff.

3. **ENTREPRENEUR SPIRIT.** I instilled in my team the concept of being fully committed to the mission. This is not easy for a generation who believes in overnight success.

4. **ESSENCE.** I established core values for the team that I framed as the "MOE-Essence": (1) maintain a high level of technical competence; (2) implement with fidelity; (3) demonstrate a spirit of cooperation and collaboration; (4) commit to personal growth and professional development; and (5) have the courage to take risks with integrity.

5. **EMPOWERMENT.** I had to learn the distinction between enabling, entitling, and empowering employees and sub-contractors.

6. **EVALUATION.** I developed a performance evaluation model that included measurement of staffs' soft skills, technical competencies, and growth potential.

7. **EMOTIONAL INTELLIGENCE.** I learned to engage my team on four (4) dimensions: (1) heart; (2) heads; (3) hands; and (4) habits.

8. **ENGAGING.** I engaged my team on: (1) what to do (knowledge); (2) why to do (mission); (3) how to do it (skills), and (4) when to do it (project management).

9. **EXPOSURE AND EXPLORATION.** I exposed young people to diverse aspects of the business of public health.

10. **ENTHUSIASM.** I had to ignite enthusiasm at every level of execution to inspire employees and partners to believe in "why we do what we do".

"Dream teams need transformational leaders for the challenges, changes, and crises on the road to success."

Dr. Quinn Motivates

Now let's Go!

CHAPTER 7

DO YOU HAVE A GROWTH AND MAINTENANCE PLAN?

You must grow the top line and maintain the bottom line.

> *"If you have not led a team through a crisis complete with internal threats to your integrity and systems and external forces aiming missiles at all your competitive advantages and resources then you have not mastered the art of execution."*
>
> Dr. Quinn Motivates

The concept of growth and maintenance in entrepreneurship is the most difficult for entrepreneurs to grasp, and ultimately master. The only way I can describe the intersection of growth and maintenance is that for most entrepreneurs, this is where "the rubber meets the road" or in some cases, where "all hell breaks loose." Over the years, I have witnessed many entrepreneurs simply give up during the growth and maintenance phase. To survive the growth and maintenance phase, you will need to become competent in leading people, managing projects, monitoring protocols and policy, launching new products and services, and growing profits all at the same time.

How to "maintain multiple lanes" during the growth and maintenance phase. The growth and maintenance process assumes you have completed the work to lay a strong foundation as outlined in chapters one (1) through six (6). The strategic business advice for maintaining and growing your enterprise requires that: (1) you are fully committed and competent as an entrepreneur; (2) you have a brand management plan in place; (3) all your "DASH" boards from chapter five (5) are fully functioning; and (4) you have a dream team strategy to quickly accommodate human resource needs as the business grows. Balancing growth and maintenance responsibilities require you to be able to switch lanes quickly. In the drive towards entrepreneurial goals, you will have to "maintain multiple lanes" as follows: (1) people-centered; (2) infrastructure-centered; (3) marketing and brand management systems; (4) growth-centered; and (5) personal life and priorities.

Lane 1: People-centered. When you reach the phase of growth and maintenance, the reality is you need competent, committed, and courageous people in play. As you prepare to grow, understand from the beginning that your employees' trust level typically drops to extreme lows as changes are introduced into a system to which they have become accustomed. They interpret unpopular decisions and events as solid evidence that you as the entrepreneur care more about yourself than you do the employees. They will internalize every piece of information and point of communication as personal. Right or wrong, you will need tough skin to let the water cooler talk run its course. Your job is to focus on aligning the existing business with future growth potential in such a way that the people who can see the big picture and want to commit will do so. Invest your time with that group. Unfortunately, you will face the fact that some people will have to exit along the aggressive growth stretch of highway. However, in the spirit of giving people on your team every opportunity to go further along the pursuit, here are some strategies for being "people-centered" during the growth and maintenance phase. There are at least five (5) different aspects of "people engagement" you must plan to work through during the growth and maintenance phase as listed below.

1. *Human resources.* Managing human resources as your company goes from "good to great" is one of the most difficult and draining decisions in the life of an authentic entrepreneur. Prepare yourself and your systems to make quicker decisions about hiring. Go back and study the human resources dashboard number three (3) in chapter five (5). Also, be prepared emotionally and legally to transition some people, some of whom may have been excellent employees in the start-up phase. However, they may not be the best for the growth phase because many will feel entitled to continue operating under the conditions and systems that existed when they started, and are less willing to yield to changes that diminish some of the perks that came with a smaller operation.

2. *Workforce training and development.* In order to grow your team, you will need to be intentional and innovative about

opportunities for on-the-job-training. This is a tricky situation as people will say they want to grow, but really they want you to finance their growth plan with them having very little "skin in the game" while you take risks to teach them new skills or pay for training. Most employees will want training and development integrated into their current 40-hour work week. Moreover, they tend to be very insensitive to the illegality of such an arrangement if they are assigned to client billable hour projects. Be up front with training and development agreements in terms of time and methods of payback for training you finance should they leave the company prior to the agreed-upon time for remaining after completing the training so that the company gets a return on its investment. If employees are not willing to meet the agreement stipulations for training and development, leave them in a maintenance position and let them do the mundane. Never force a person to grow.

3. *Leadership development.* Leadership development is vital for growth. As you observe your team performing under different operating conditions, pay close attention to individuals' ability to communicate effectively, as well as their potential to motivate and manage others. Prior to making decisions on investing in leadership development, engage those with potential in very candid conversations about balancing their current work-load, work-life priorities, and their own willingness to invest time and energy into growing into a leadership position. Be sure that you stop short of guaranteeing a salary increase or promotion, however you can promise an assessment and a decision date to consider such changes if they embark upon leadership development opportunities. You may benefit from revisiting my 25 core elements of teaming in chapter six (6) paying close attention to the final element on "moving managers to leaders". Finally, I also recommend reading my book titled *"Leadership Matters"* to get a grasp on what a comprehensive approach to leadership

development entails in terms of mastering core competencies needed for leadership and management.

4. *Teaming agreements.* Your growth plan should prompt you to explore opportunities for new teaming arrangements. Prior to solidifying any new agreements, review the advantages and disadvantages of teaming agreements as outlined in chapter six (6), option two (2) for human resources strategies. Review the teaming agreement advantages and disadvantages. Update existing MOUs and teaming agreement templates to reflect your growth strategy as opposed to what worked during the start-up phase.

5. *Strategic advisors.* As you gear up for growth, consider formalizing and even incentivizing a seasoned team of strategic advisors to serve as consultants for providing feedback on your initial growth plan, as well as during the execution phase. You could also form a "CEO Mentoring Group" where a team of CEOs provide each other with feedback as part of a self-managed cohort of sole-proprietors with diverse skills and competencies.

Lane 2: Infrastructure-centered. Prior to moving into the fast lane of growth, you want to examine thoroughly your business and operating infrastructure to be sure it is sound and can absorb the growth model as it unfolds.

1. *General business operations and administration.* Review your current general and operating procedures and systems as a first prompting of what might be obsolete or need to change to better manage and monitor the way the organization is destined to evolve as your growth process manifests.

2. *Finance and accounting.* As your growth process may include empowering others to be held accountable for managing resources and budgets, be sure you review your finance and accounting protocols to be sure that managers have the appropriate authority to achieve results requiring access to funds. You also want checks and balances to guard against theft and mismanagement. You may also benefit from teaching managers how to analyze and make

decisions using profit and loss statements and cash flow statements as a starting point for being fiscally responsible for their projects.

3. *Continued Quality Improvement (CQI).* As you prepare to be more consumed with growth, think about how you can institutionalize quality assurance checkpoints for goods and services in a way that staff and partners can anticipate your time and attention to the details of their projects. Also incorporate opportunities to praise your maintenance team for doing things right as you hunt for new business. Oftentimes, morale is lowered unnecessarily among those "doing their job" when they see all the accolades and positive news and feedback being given to those on growth projects.

4. *Information systems/technology upgrades.* In simple terms, your growth plan may result in a need for technological upgrades. Be sure you assess and budget for purchasing new hardware, software, and other gadgets that help increase performance overall.

Lane 3: Marketing and brand management system. For most entrepreneurs, up until the first phase of growth, marketing and branding has been your responsibility. Now you must invest in competent brand managers who can apply the comprehensive brand management system for entrepreneurship in chapter four (4). Be sure that the individual tapped for this position understands that brand management in an entrepreneurial environment entails more than just the "four (4) Ps of marketing" undergirding the traditional marketing mix formula. Remember to formulate a job description that reflects all the functions of a competent brand manager, as well as managing core components of your marketing and sales dashboard as outlined in chapter five (5). Other preparatory work in reworking your marketing and sales system for growth opportunities include reviewing key accounts and relationships, updating your corporate capabilities statements, as well as updating your credentials for key staff and partners. Finally, as you gear up the full team for growth and maintenance, reiterate that directly and indirectly, everyone is responsible for marketing and sales.

Lane 4: Growth-centered. Once your brand management system has been established, you will need to shift gears and devise a plan for growth. You can begin with revisiting your start-up business plan, but remember that you are in motion now and much of what you penned in your original business plan was theoretical and forecasting. Now you have some actual data, insight, and lived experiences to guide your growth. Therefore, when you think about growth planning, focus on taking your initial business and marketing plan to the next level, and not rewriting your business plan per' se. Growth strategies are different for every product, service, or brand portfolio, and are driven by market demand, and industry trends and standards. That being said, there are some universal principles of growth that you must adhere to, commonly referred to as strategic planning, sustainability, or succession planning.

1. *Mission statement.* Revisit your mission statement and determine if your purpose and aspirations for being in business remain the same as when you started the company. If they are not, you need to do the work to either change your mission statement to match the overall business goals or change your strategic thrust to fit the original mission statement.

2. *Vision statement.* If your company is more than three (3) years old, then you need to revisit the vision of what your company will look like in five (5) or more years. If you have achieved that which your vision statement aimed for, it may indicate your original vision was too small. This time, for your growth plan, think bigger, broader, and bolder.

3. *Core values and guiding principles.* The core values are the guiding principles that dictate behavior and action. Prior to embarking upon a growth strategy, I highly recommend that you revisit your core values as they serve as the foundation upon which you perform and engage diverse stakeholders. Remember that your core values reflect your bedrock character as a person and as an entrepreneur and should remain constant no matter the volatility in the marketplace. You also need to be

sure your teaming partners and employees are clear on the core values and guiding principles.

4. *Environmental scan.* No matter how busy you think you are, you need to take time to scan the external environment that impacts your organization and brand. Specifically, an external or macro-environmental scan is an analysis of the external conditions that you need factored into your growth planning process. There are at least six (6) areas that you should monitor: political, economic, social, technological, legal, and environmental. As you conduct your research, ask yourself, what has changed in my external environment that impacts my operating systems, employees, products or services directly or indirectly, as well as favorably or unfavorably?

5. *Consumer marketing research.* If your growth plan involves creating new products or services, or brand extensions of existing offerings in your portfolio, you will need to conduct consumer marketing research. This includes gathering hard data, as well as softer stories that may be captured via social media. The key is to understand the extent to which your new product or service is solving a consumer-driven problem.

6. *SWOT.* A SWOT is an acronym for "strengths, weaknesses, opportunities, and threats". A SWOT is a simple analysis for documenting your company's current situation in each of the four (4) categories of a SWOT analysis. For strengths and weakness, you are primarily taking a critical look inside your organization. For threats and opportunities, you are using external environmental scan perspectives and consumer marketing research data to identify opportunities in the market place and threats to your growth and maintenance strategy that must be addressed as you drive forward.

7. *Competitive advantage.* As you gear up for growth, you want to be very clear on what are your competitive advantages. There is no such thing in business as "we have no competition." If you are unable to identify direct competition, then pinpoint

indirect competition. Another way to think about competitive advantage is to consider what you can do to capitalize on, perhaps being the first to market or providing some innovative feature or benefit to an existing product or service. However, never under-estimate that competition is on the horizon; it may be closer than you think in terms of enterprising partners and employees soaking up your knowledge and approach. This is why non-compete clauses, and confidentiality agreements must be part of standard operating procedures.

8. ***Long-term strategic objectives.*** For your long-term objectives, focus on a three-year time period. I suggest no more than five (5) concrete objectives that focus on what it would take to achieve your vision. Each of the five (or less) broad objectives should then have its own set of strategies, shorter term priorities, action items, and financial performance measures. Keep in mind that strategies, priorities, and actions are dynamic and must be managed in appropriate time intervals. Your job as the chief business growth officer is to lead the growth team through changes as deemed necessary to achieve the overall objective, and most of all the financial results sought.

9. ***Strategies.*** Strategies point to the general direction you plan to move in terms of getting from "concept to market." Growth strategy begins with idea generation, then transition to identifying people, process, and action plans that tie back to the long-term objectives. Unlike your initial business planning period where most entrepreneurs tend to work alone, growth strategies should be documented with every detail and decision possible, so that you can put a sound project or brand manager in charge of driving for results.

10. ***Short-term goals/priorities/initiatives.*** Once you have a solid strategy in place, you need to convert those strategic objectives into specific performance targets. This is where you want to be clear on what the growth objective entails, when it

will be achieved, who is responsible for managing the progress, and ultimately achieving the results that fall within the one- to two-year time horizon.

11. *Action items/plans.* Action items and plans constitute what I call "tactical take-downs". Tactical take-downs are defined as tasks performed at the operations level aimed at advancing the broader business strategy. Everything listed as action items must include a person who is responsible for executing and a due date of completion. The key word is "execution" when it comes to tactical take-downs.

12. *Dashboard indicators.* In chapter five (5), I provided a glimpse of seven (7) different dash boards that serve as your business gauge and navigation system. Dashboard six (6) alerted you to begin thinking about your continued growth strategy using my version of a "SMART" growth model. At this phase of growth and maintenance, select a few key performance indicators and align them with your short-term goals and action plans, then track your performance against monthly targets to achieve measurable results.

13. *Financial performance.* In gearing up for growth, you want to use your own financial statements, as compared to industry data to set financial performance goals. This background analysis should be rather easy to locate if you did the work to maintain lane number two (2) related to finance and accounting systems maintenance. Based on historical records and future projections, this assessment helps plan and predict the future, allowing you to gain much better control over your organization's financial performance.

14. *New program/service development plan.* If your growth strategy includes a new product or service, you will need to develop a detailed plan for moving it from concept, to start-up, to full growth. The reason you must thoroughly document at this critical juncture is because you will be stretched between growth and maintenance, and you will need to rely upon your

team's ability to read and comprehensive the full execution plan and move forward without your daily oversight. If written to specific details, you can appoint a brand manager or project manager to oversee the full execution. If you decide to move forward without a detailed plan, you are setting yourself up for problems.

15. *Growth through acquisition or new teaming agreements.* An often overlooked opportunity for growth is to acquire a competitor or collaborative partner. As you have been working with promising partners, another viable growth strategy might be to acquire portions of their goods and services rather than spend time and resources developing them in house. Of course this strategy has advantages and disadvantages, but depending upon your growth plan, it may make sense as opposed to spending time and money on building a product or service from concept to market only to compete with those you may be able to cooperate with in the marketplace.

16. *Dissolution.* Part of growth is to stop doing what is not working or making you money and just eating up cash and time so you can free up those resources to pursue more profitable opportunities. Prior to embarking upon a growth strategy, review your existing portfolio in comparison to your original marketing plan and financial pro-formas. Once determined that a product or service is under-performing against plan, with no uptick in sales or profit on the horizon, you may have to do a close out so you can focus on growth.

*Lane 5: **Personal life and priorities.*** The entrepreneur's overall state of health and wellness is paramount to the growth of the company. As the leader of your business endeavors, it is imperative that you conduct a thorough health and wellness check on yourself. In addition to annual wellness visits, be sure to schedule age- and gender-appropriate tests. Also, revisit your fun, faith, and distress activities. If you are not enjoying the journey, then don't be afraid to think exit strategy rather than growth strategy.

Expect pebbles to pop-up and prick your windshield as you drive long stretches of highway. As long as they don't impair your vision, keep driving. But if ever a bigger boulder is hurled at you and shatters your view, thereby making it dangerous for you to drive, don't be afraid to park the proverbial car and repair the damage. In this case the metaphor is about those personal life priorities that cannot be compromised. You will read about them in chapter nine (9) where I identify eight (8) pillars of priorities that include: faith, family, friends, followers, financial planning, fitness, fun, and future.

To maximize growth in general, you need a team that is fast acting and fast thinking to respond to new business opportunities. You also need a team that is meticulous in maintaining the work and serving the customers you already have. But as the leader of both teams, it is your responsibility to be sure that these teams understand that, while they have different gifts, and talents, and areas of expertise, they are all on the same team striving towards the same mission. No matter which sub-team they are placed on, whether growth or maintenance, you need to make it clear that every team member must learn and practice key principles of sales and marketing.

MY "DRIVING" LESSONS LEARNED

IN GROWING NEW BUSINESS AND MAINTAINING EXISTING BUSINESS

1. **"The TUCKMAN MODEL,"** I applied "Tuckman's model of organizational change to make sense of key phases of growth that he termed: forming, storming, norming, and performing.

2. **TECHNICALLY TIGHT.** I institutionalized comprehensive technical standards to assure that staff and sub-contractors excelled as high performing expert consultants.

3. **TIME.** I coached my teams on the concept of "time," including time management, timelines, and timing.

4. **TEAMWORK.** I learned to leave the "shop floor" and trust that staff and sub-contractors would apply the tools and strategies made available to them to emerge as a high-peforming team independent of my day-to-day oversight.

5. **TASKS.** I shifted from managing and monitoring by the hour to by the tasks primarily due to the unprecedented take-over of social media and other personal distractions in our society.

6. **TOUGH TIMES.** I pushed through tough times as I grew and maintained my business. Tough times included financial, human resource-related, and personal crises for me, as well as for my team.

7. **TENSION.** I learned to spring into problem solving mode at the least little bit of tension. This was especially valuable in working with passive-aggressive team members.

8. **TOUCH BASE.** I integrated formal and informal touch bases into the monitoring system where I review techniques and tactics, but also reiterate the mission and vision and how each smaller task contributes to the bigger picture.

9. **TROUBLE.** I learned to detect and confront "trouble", including poor performance, lack of a teaming spirit, and unethical and illegal practices. I also monitor my "stars" who, sometimes slip into ego trips.

10. **TRANSITION.** I learned to transition people "up or out" at a faster pace due to limited resources. I designed a leadership development track to transition promising employees into leadership roles; and I grew a thicker skin for releasing people when there was less promise for transferring skills, or transitioning them up in the company.

"Don't let the odds and obstacles intimidate you."

Dr. Quinn Motivates

Now Let's Go!

CHAPTER 8
CAN YOU ACCEPT FAILURE AS PART OF THE PROCESS?

Let failure be the fuel that drives you forward when you feel like giving up.

> *"The fear of failure is a fatal disease that has killed more dreams than we care to count."*
>
> Dr. Quinn Motivates

When it comes to entrepreneurship you must have the courage to take full responsibility for the failures that come with the process. What others call failure, entrepreneurs call "moving forward". In our culture we don't even like to verbalize the word "failure" because it implies a waste of time and money, and perhaps implies incompetence or a lack of talent. Furthermore, people who fail are labeled as losers and are held suspect to character flaws that may have caused them to fail.

The inspiration for this chapter came from my own experiences in having to get back up after failing hard. I remember every detail of the successes from 2005 to 2007 as I sat in my basement and wrote and won eight (8) multi-year contracts in a row! We were so successful that I took on the liability of a $60,000.00 operating cost of office space in the prestigious Buckhead business district in Atlanta. Just as we began to press forward in building a cohesive dream team with a comprehensive body of work comprising all four (4) practice areas, we lost 13 proposals in a row. While I didn't have to fire anyone or downsize the office space, I do recall being overwhelmed as my confidence was shattered for a season. The most anxiety I experienced was in owning my responsibility for paying decent salaries to college-educated staff, most of whom were just graduating from either undergraduate or graduate school under a mountain of student loan debt, becoming first-time home owners, driving luxury cars, setting wedding dates, and caring for young children. Adding to my stress level was the fact that I was married to a conservative business man who was risk averse in any shape, form, or fashion. You can only imagine the level of conflict that my business failings sparked on a personal level.

Being the historian and sociologist that I am, I did what brings me pleasure and lowers my stress. I launched my own research project on the phenomenon of failure in our culture. What I concluded is that our society has socially-constructed failure as something to be avoided at all cost and under all circumstances. We reinforce the need to avoid failure by sanctioning behaviors that encourage us to avoid, hide, or minimize failure. My theory on why Americans are afraid to fail is imbedded in an examination of key socializing agents that reinforce our quest to avoid failure at all costs.

1. *Family* teaches us to hide failure from the outside world to avoid shaming the family name. Ultimately, we are governed by family secrets and the privatization of troubles.

2. *School* teaches us to avoid failure even if it means cheating among every group of stakeholders involved in the education of a child, including students, teachers, administrators, and parent(s.) Parents in particular reinforce that it is unacceptable to fail by doing homework and school projects on one hand, and having harsh punishments for poor report cards on the other.

3. *Dance/Sports* teaches us to quit if we are not very good or a natural at a particular sport at a certain age of competition even though there are still transferable skills and life lessons to be learned from simply being on the team.

4. *Organized religion* teaches us to equate failing with sinning. Moral failure is met with public shaming, confessions, and formal ex-communication rituals.

5. *The workforce* teaches us that failure is equivalent with incompetence. In addition, the price for failure in the workforce typically is being fired, which then sparks off a set of failures in one's personal life. As such, the motive to avoid failure means many talented employees opt to remain in mid-management as opposed to taking on greater leadership roles and responsibilities that include more risks by nature.

What I now understand after experiencing failures and setbacks is that authentic entrepreneurs see failure totally different from the rest of the world. Until I faced failure square in the face personally and professionally, I really didn't know what I was truly capable of achieving. I learned how to survive when my back was against the wall, and when resources were scarce, and the odds of keeping the dream alive seemed insurmountable.

As you grow as an authentic entrepreneur you will constantly come into contact with failure. Of course failure carries with it the potential for destruction and surely it can rip the heart of an entrepreneur and kill the spirit. An alternative is to use failure as fuel to fire you and your team up in anticipation of a brighter future. I suggest you make friends with failure and learn how to peacefully co-exist with it. To help in this regard I have identified 12 steps for making friends with failure. The first six (6) steps are about using very private moments to recover from failure. Think of the first phase as putting the proverbial car in the shop and getting some major repairs after an accident. Not only did the car you were driving get hit hard, but perhaps you got banged up and bruised and you need time to heal. The last six (6) steps center on facing the public and getting back on the road to pursue your entrepreneurial destiny.

"Dr. Quinn's 12- Steps for Making Friends with Failure"

Step 1: Feel it. Build a tolerance for experiencing a full range of emotions after a major setback while resisting the need to attack, blame, or medicate the pain. Allowing yourself to go through a full range of emotions is the best way to assure that you do not suppress negativity that can stifle your push forward. Give yourself permission to sit alone with the failure as a way to make peace with the reality that things really did fall apart. Don't run from it. Own the failure. Release the anger. Don't hide in shame. Get rid of the guilt and embarrassment. Push away any thoughts that it was a waste of time and money. Instead, internalize what you learned and reflect upon how your values, character, and integrity were tested. Assess damage that may have been done to relationships you value and have every intention of repairing. Mourn the loss of those relationships that you know in your heart may not survive. Absorb the sadness as a sign that you are human and really care about the people impacted by the failure.

Learn to let hurtful moments pass through you and not manifest in you. Pause, rest, take a deep breath, relax, do something that reminds you that you are human, and then laugh at yourself. Accept that while failure does not feel good, it will all work out for your good. As you feel your way through the failure, remember that it is not what knocked you down, but rather what is motivating you to get up that will make all the difference in terms of how you rebound from the failure.

Step 2: Focus. Focus on your strengths, talents, skills, and resources. If you did the work in step one (1) to feel a full range of emotions as a way to stabilize your feelings, then you are ready to focus. Clear your conscience. Get your mind right. Remind yourself of what you can do and figure out how to redirect your efforts to be able to do more of what you are good at and passionate about. With a renewed mind, think about new ways to solve the problems that led to failure. Focus on new opportunities and strategies to rebound.

Step 3: Fellowship. Remain committed to a personal relationship with God through prayer, meditation, biblical study, fellowshipping, and serving in ministry. By default, failure tends to shake one's faith. We often ask ourselves, perhaps internally, "where was God in all this?" In recovering from failure you have do the work to understand what your faith says about failure and the role of the Divine in the process. From a spiritual perspective I came to see failure as a test to strengthen and prepare me for the next level of growth and responsibility. It also reinforced that no matter what, I would remain committed to a personal relationship with God through prayer, meditation, biblical study, fellowship with other believers, and serve in ministry. Working through my faith allowed me to be at peace deep within my soul about the meaning and purpose of failure.

Step 4: Face Fears. Accept fear as a constant companion. The thing about fear is it shows up uniquely designed as those areas in life where you lack faith for moving forward or have bad past memories of failure. As you step out on faith in pursuit of your purpose, fear will set it. Fear can become a giant that keeps you from making the first step or it can become a paralysing force that freezes you at the very thought of failure.

Step 5: Forgive. Forgive yourself and others for negative thoughts, words, or actions that may have been exchanged. Let's face it. Failure can trigger some words and actions that are hurtful to others. Some things are said or done out of character. This is why asking for forgiveness must be part of rebounding from failure. Forgiveness is placed in the middle of the 12-step to recovering from failure because it is necessary to work through some alone-time before you begin to interact with others about what may have transpired during the failure.

Step 6: Free yourself. No matter the shape, form, or magnitude, you must free yourself from all limitations. As you prepare to get moving again after experiencing a major setback, identify all the factors that could get in the way of your getting back on the road. Remember that the garage door is about to come up and you are about to take to the road again and you need your driveway clear! Remove all real and perceived "buts", "butt", "barriers", "boundaries", and "barricades". The "buts" are characterized as the mental doubts and blocks imposed. The "butt" refers to the need to move again physically. Barriers are those blockages that are imposed by others directly or indirectly to either stop you from starting again, or at a minimum, make it a bit more difficult. Boundaries are those limits that are in the social environments where you live, work, play, or love. Finally, you have to free yourself from the "barricades" which are defined as those systemic and historical hindrances, such as racism, sexism, or ageism or any form of discrimination that makes it harder for you to pursue your dream.

Step 7: Fire-up. You have to fire yourself up. Start the engine. Turn on your motivational music from your inspirational soundtrack. Get your mind back in the game. Re-recruit your team. Solidify and execute your comeback strategy. Go back and revisit the authentic enthusiasm chapter in this book. Find "inspirational others" to lean on. Prepare a "tactical take-down" list of actions you can complete in 30 days, then 90 days, and then 6-months. Eliminate distractions and discard unnecessary weight, including emotional, physical, administrative, and humans who are too heavy to carry. These small wins will restore your morale and self-confidence that you are "driven." Make rapid decisions that are consistent with your value system and goals.

Step 8: Fight. Fight for what you believe is your life's purpose. Once you decide to face your failures and try again, be prepared for the fight of your life. Even though you have done substantial work up to this point to put failure in a proper perspective, the minute you resolve to try again is the exact time you will experience another round of doubt. You will have to fight. You have to fight past your own negative self-talk. You have to fight past the naysayers and skeptics. You have to learn to roll with the punches and not fold under pressure. I devised what I call my "fight plan" which includes "pray, plan, press, and repeat this process." As you vow to fight for your hopes and dreams you develop something called "fortitude," which is defined as having the strength of character, courage, and confidence to pursue your purpose. Fortitude helps you stand on your convictions that you are an authentic entrepreneur in moments of conflict, confusion, and unprecedented controversy.

Step 9: Face it and Fix it. When you resolve to fight, you need to spend some time fixing what went wrong. Most failures have a list of negative consequences, including diverse types of relationships that need mending. Face everyone involved and every situation with dignity. Hold your head up and do the best you can to fix all that went bump in the night as things perhaps spiraled out of control. Listen to how the failure impacted others. Help them recover to the extent possible and as resources allow. Review every task, resource, and critical path more rigorously now that you have some lived and learned experiences under your belt in terms of "what didn't go well." Determine what new actions, options, and strategies should be utilized for the comeback. Bring finite closure to that which continues to threaten your success.

Step 10: Finish. Finish what you started or what you failed at even if it's late. Before you move forward, finish any outstanding business that fell through the cracks. If you owe people or vendors for supplies, pay your bills. If you promised products and services to clients and customers, make good on your promise. Understand that not everyone will be receptive to your gestures and efforts to make them whole because when you do so, you rob them of their victim story and need to cling to some negative narrative related to watching you fail. Make peace that you did what was humanly possible to finish as a test of your character and integrity. Interestedly enough, if you explore all factors, often times those with the loudest negativity typically contributed to the firm's failure by either not doing their job or not being committed to the journey in the first place. In any case, once you have taken care of the people who relied upon your detriment during the failure, then vow to finish stronger and fail better next time.

Step 11: Forward. Don't allow failure to stand in the way of taking on new risks. In moving forward you must take full responsibility for all the consequences and aftermath associated with failure. You cannot afford to wallow in self-pity or shame. You have to get up and get moving again. Don't assassinate yourself because of mistakes. You have to operate out of a spirit of moving forward. Going forward also means carrying lessons learned with you; and constantly ask, "What is going to be different going forward?"

Step 12: Fail better. Immerse yourself in the stories of famous people who failed better. Include more than just entrepreneurs in this instance. I have developed what I call my "fail better hall of fame". My study of successful people transcends race, gender, and areas of expertise as I have examined the lives of high-achieving entrepreneurs, corporate executives, politicians, religious leaders, government officials, award-winning journalists and writers, record-setting sports legends, platinum-producing entertainers, and compassionate civic and community advocates. In reading and reflecting upon these individuals' lives, I discovered that they view failure differently than most in our society. Rather than see failure as a finite sign to quit and do something different, they figure out how to fail better.

FAMOUS PEOPLE WHO FAILED TO BECOME BETTER

#	Name	#	Name	#	Name	#	Name
1.	Oprah Winfrey	11.	Steve Harvey	21.	Tyler Perry	31.	Zane Grey
2.	Henry Ford	12.	Sidney Poitier	22.	President Barak Obama	32.	Mark Cuban
3.	Michael Jordan	13.	J.K. Rowling	23.	Dr. Martin Luther King Jr.	33.	President Jimmy Carter
4.	Steve Jobs	14.	Will Smith	24.	Fred Astaire	34.	Kerry Washington
5.	R.H. Macy	15.	Steven Spielberg	25.	Winston Churchill	35.	Mary Kay Ashe
6.	Bill Gates	16.	Dr. Seuss	26.	Suze Orman	36.	Berry Gordy
7.	Harland David Sanders	17.	Michael Bloomberg	27.	Iyanla Vanzant	37.	Cathy Hughes
8.	Walt Disney	18.	Larry King	28.	Barbara Corcoran	38.	Sheila Johnson
9.	Thomas Edison	19.	Vera Wang	29.	Gary Zukav	39.	Vanessa Williams
10.	Orville and Wilbur Wright	20.	Bernie Mac	30.	Abraham Lincoln	40.	Serena Williams

WHAT "FAMOUS FAILURES" HAVE IN COMMON

Here is a list of common themes among high achievers in general (and not just entrepreneurs) in the aftermath of failure:

1. They accept failure as a normal part of the path to success.
2. They never lost self-confidence in their ability to reach a goal.
3. They remained grounded in a strong sense of purpose.
4. They didn't make excuses or blame others for having failed.

5. They took great measures to perfect variables that contributed to failure.
6. They were not afraid to re-invent themselves.
7. They work extremely hard to recover, regroup, recommit, and rebound.
8. They have a thick skin in accepting unfair hits and criticism.
9. They knew when to defend and when to keep it moving.
10. They were not afraid to be even more radical or aggressive in the turn-around strategy.

My final perspective on failure is that no matter how prepared you are, how many steps you take in the right direction, failure remains a real possibility at some point along your pursuit. Sometimes you will feel like you are standing still or running in place, or going in circles. At this very moment you must not give up. You must not give in. You must decide that your dream, your goal, your purpose is absolutely worth giving it all you got. Some people will make subtle hints. Others will broadcast it loud and clear that maybe it's time to try something else and be content with the fact that at least you tried. You must continue on. As you do due diligence, you will discover that people stole from you, took advantage of you, cheated the process, cut corners, and most of all lacked the commitment needed to succeed in the first place. You must move forward. Slip past the stumbling blocks. Outmaneuver the obstacles. Make no mistakes about it, there will be moments when you feel lost, defeated, bewildered, battered, and simply broken beyond comprehension. You must believe that you can do it again and do it better this time. You will feel lonely and discouraged as you witness the doubters and haters do what they do. Resolve to never dissolve your dream, for if you stop dreaming, then you will surely experience hopelessness at every wicked twist and turn in your pursuit of entrepreneurship. Get back in the "driver's seat." Buckle up. Put it in overdrive... *And Let's Go!*

MY "DRIVING" LESSONS LEARNED
IN FAILING BETTER

1. **FEEL IT.** I allowed myself to experience a full range of emotions. Initially I resorted to my numbing activities of eating and shopping and when that didn't make me feel better, I mustered up the courage to sit with my feelings and make sense of how failure had impacted me from the inside out.

2. **FAMOUS FAILURES.** During the process of reconciling my feelings, I reviewed inspirational stories of others who experienced major failures and used them as launching pads to win big.

3. **FALLING APART.** I became comfortable with the falling apart process as I began to view it as a way of releasing people who no longer contributed to the overall purpose of my entrepreneurial pursuit.

4. **FOCUS.** I focused in on what I did well and figured out how to position myself to do more of what I was excellent at doing and enjoyed doing.

5. **FELLOWSHIP.** I shared my failures and feelings about failure with my key confidants within the body of Christ.

6. **FACED MY FEARS.** I immersed myself in a therapeutic process where for the first time I came face to face with what I was really afraid of: (1) rejection and abandonment, and (2) losing. Of course these fears go back to childhood. However, once I let go of the need to hold on to people who wanted to go and re-purposed losing as learning, I felt free to pursue my goals with dignity and integrity.

7. **FORGIVE.** I went through a spiritual cleansing process where I released everyone from blame for my failures. This actually resulted in a kind of personal freedom that is unexplainable.

8. **FRIENDS AND FAMILY.** After letting go of some of those "who meant me no harm, but did me no good either," I leaned hard on my real friends and family as a support system.

9. **FIRED-UP.** I relied upon my history and track record of winning and used it to bounce back and get back in the game to start again and finish stronger than ever.

10. **FAIL BETTER.** I resolved the fact that if I was going to achieve anything signifcant in this lifetime then I needed to make friends with failure and learn how to fail better on my way to greater!

"Get ready to fail better."

Dr. Quinn Motivates

Now let's Go!

CHAPTER 9

DO YOU HAVE A PROPER PERSPECTIVE ON YOUR PRIORITIES?

Value and honor your agreements.

"Reprogram yourself to replace work-life balance with prioritization."
Dr. Quinn Motivates

I was serving on a panel of women entrepreneurs to inspire and motivate a group of potential business owners to take the leap of faith and start their business. During the question and answer portion of the program a woman stood up and posed the question to all the panelists, "How do you address your need for work-life balance?" Despite the high energy and quick on our feet answers from the last 45 minutes, none of the other panelists wanted to go first in responding to this question. I courageously took to the podium and said, "The reality is that work-life balance as it has been conceptualized in our society is in-consistent with the entrepreneurial lifestyle. This means that at every phase and stage of business development, relationships you value the most will be tested. The truth of the matter is when we try to function within a work-life balance frame of reference we fail miserably because we are on 24/7."

The conceptual framing for this paradigm of prioritization grew out of my reading Stephen Covey's book "First Things First," where he took principle number one (1) from his book "7 Habits of Highly Effective People" and expounded upon it. The core of "First Things First", according to Stephen Covey, is that true productivity is not about getting more things done in less time, but rather doing things that matter with the time you have. As I explored this core concept, I realized that authentic entrepreneurs must re-program ourselves to move from thinking "work-life balance" to "prioritization." Instead, focus on honoring your agreements within the context of priorities. I have identified eight (8) pillars of priorities that I sometimes refer to as my "pillows" because when any of my priorities are not in order, I find myself being a bit restless, and to the other extreme, unable to sleep at night.

"8 Pillars of Priorities"

Pillar 1: Faith. Authentic entrepreneurs typically are people of faith. For the most part, I personally have worked with those who believe in Christianity. However, I have come to respect the commitment to faith I observe in other entrepreneurs who are committed to Judaism, Islam, Buddhism, and Hinduism. In fact, while studying abroad as an exchange student to Israel my junior year of high school, I witnessed Jews and Muslims literally close their stores "religiously" every day for a few hours to spend time in prayer and meditation.

As a former Mary Kay Beauty Consultant, I am equally encouraged by Mary Kay's creed of "God first, Family Second, and Career Third." However, the most inspiring story of prioritizing one's faith is S. Truett Cathy, founder of Chick Fil A, who not only closed all his stores on Sundays, but he also taught Sunday School for 50 years. Imagine the false sense of security his decision to be closed one day on a weekend sent to competitors in the fast food industry. As you mature in faith and as your business model transforms over time, you will need to work through how you prioritize activities associated with your faith, including fellowship and worship, prayer and meditation, and mission work to be of service to others.

Pillar 2: Family. Authentic entrepreneurs make time for family. Once you embark upon the pursuit of entrepreneurship, however, the old model of "work-life balance" has to be renegotiated for something more relevant and appropriate as the 9-5 workday gives way to less predictable hours of work engagement. I suggest making a list of family members and key family events and activities that are non-negotiable. Place those on the schedule and block that time out as unavailable for business. If you have an intimate partner, prioritize spending time together, and establish rituals and promises you know you can fulfill. When you are with family, be fully engaged in the activities and conversations of the family. The key is to be disciplined enough to shut down business for a finite time. However, if you must take a business call or work on a project, communicate as much in advance, so your family anticipates your being unavailable for some short period of time.

If at all possible, include your family in small, short-term activities for your business as a way of including them in your life and sharing with them in real time what you are working on. This is especially rewarding for children who are eager to help out and learn. Also, if your business is co-owned with a spouse, set family priorities around being fully present during holidays, birthdays, graduations, extracurricular activities, and performances. Even if you must steal away on vacation for a few hours to do work, never be missing for long periods of time. The point is that when you lock and load a family priority onto the schedule, be courageous enough to say no to business opportunities that would cause you to have to break the commitment.

Pillar 3: Friends. As our society uses the term "friend" so loosely in today's world of social media, prioritizing friends can be a bit more complicated. By friend, I am referring to that sacred inner-circle of friends who probably are more like family. This set of friends is not to be confused with professorial networks. In fact, I challenge you to write down your top 10 "friends" and document the length of time you have known them, and what you value about the friendship. I also suggest using this time to consider what you give to and what you get from each friend. Write down how you typically communicate and interact with each and how that might evolve as your business grows. Highlight their birthdays, anniversaries, and other special days you intend to continue sharing with each. Just as with family, block those dates on the calendar as "unavailable for business." Clearly the list of "10" is arbitrary and was selected to get you thinking about who your true friends are. You may have more or less depending upon your definition of friend. For example I have a best friend since we were nine (9) and ten (10) years old who is prioritized just like family. The conflict in prioritizing "friends" is with the list of people who believe they should have made your priority list of friends. Well, I can help you work that out too, but that's another book for another day! For now, the point is to be sure you know who you count as a real friend and whose love and support you don't want to compromise as you pursue your goal of entrepreneurship.

Pillar 4: Followers. As you grow your business, you will learn who your "courageous followers are". These are the competent and committed employees, sub-contractors, and teaming partners. No doubt as you work closely with this group, bonds and emotional ties are developed that surpass the typical business relationship model. Over time, these individuals will celebrate personal and professional milestones, as well as experience tragedies and losses. It is worth spending some time determining the extent to which you can prioritize this group. Be sure this level of engagement does not become a conflict of interest, and be sure it is earned, and not viewed as a privilege. The catch in prioritizing spending time with your followers is that you must do due diligence on the front end and hire the right people for the entrepreneurial experience. In addition, they must be available for such engagement, and mature enough to be mentored and managed with minimum conflict.

For me, I prioritized my group of followers with leadership potential. People commenting on my social media postings about my interaction with staff validate that I take very good care of my team, well beyond paying them market-rate wages for their skill sets, education, experience, and potential. Beyond being fair to all from a corporate perspective, I prioritize spending quality time with my courageous followers. I spend genuine time with their families and children, including taking them on vacations, and sponsoring wellness day activities. We have dance parties, make-up and hair team builders, wine-tastings, and shopping sprees. In addition, I have been known to stretch budgets to include high performers at workshops, conferences, and speaking events in Las Vegas, Trinidad/Tobago, Washington, DC, and New York City. Also when we travel, I make sure we take time for fine dining, theatre, or other excursions, depending upon the city and what it has to offer.

Pillar 5: Financial planning. As entrepreneurs it is of the utmost importance that you prioritize planning for your future. In chapter five (5), I provided some exit strategy options for entrepreneurs that assumed that the entrepreneur had invested properly in personal financial planning. As I am in no position to endorse a particular brand, firm, or professional for financial planning, I can provide the following guidance based on my own experience. When I left corporate America I re-invested my 401-K funds into a ROTH-IRA and continued making annual contributions to my retirement fund. I attended a financial planning small group fellowship offered through my church to be sure my financial planning approach was aligned with my Christian values. I became a student of Suze Orman, whose philosophy is "people first, money second." Finally I set up some personal finance goals to establish reserves for living expenses to survive tough times, such as cash flow shortages, loss of contracts, or personal emergencies when I couldn't be billable on projects. In essence, you want to approach personal financial planning in a way that assures you have short-term options to meet obligations, mid-term options to enjoy life, and long-term options for retirement, and to leave a legacy.

Pillar 6: Fitness. You must prioritize keeping your body fit and well. I am grieved by the number of stories I hear of successful entrepreneurs who can't even enjoy the fruits of their labor due to health reasons or early deaths. Heart disease, stroke, obesity, and clinical depression are the main culprits. Even I must admit that 20 extra pounds seemed to just have come from nowhere as I embarked upon a goal of writing and self-publishing 10 books in one (1) year as my gift to myself for being in business 10 years. After six (6) months into the process, I was sluggish, sleeping more and writing less. My refrigerator and cabinets were full of comforting carbs they both were. I looked at my workout schedule and realized I hadn't seen the gym in four (4) months. I took radical measures and lost ten (10) pounds in 90 days, and the full 20 in five (5) months using a personal trainer, a 1200-calorie per day plan, and getting active in group exercise. Not only did I avoid having to buy a new wardrobe to accommodate the 20 additional pounds, but my energy increased, my endurance for speaking improved, and my mental health was greatly enhanced.

You need a workout and nutrition plan that can be easily adapted into your entrepreneurial schedule. You also need mental wellness time to clear your mind for creativity and decision-making. Every six (6) months, take a wellness week where you plan wellness visits to a general practitioner, dentist, therapist, and get any age-appropriate or lifestyle assessments completed. Also consider managing your body mass index (BMI) to help you control your weight. Be sure to program rejuvenation and rest time into your busy daily schedule. Join a fitness group or gym to break the monotony of being alone as is common among entrepreneurs. After a major project or setback, allow yourself a few days to shut down completely to reflect and replenish your energy.

Pillar 7: Fun. Enjoy the journey! One of the perks of running your own business is that ideally you should be working in an area that you are passionate about. That passion should convert to a natural kind of enjoyment that springs from a satisfaction grounded in the idea that you are living your dreams. If you are not having fun, you need to do some soul-searching to find out why you are not enjoying this journey. Be creative in your strategies to have fun within the context of living an entrepreneurial lifestyle. For example, when I am going to a great city for a conference or workshop, sometimes I arrive early or remain throughout the weekend to take advantage of opportunities to take in a show, dinner, shopping, or do a spa day. I also commit to a "play date" at least once per month where I do something that I enjoy. The point is simply to figure out what constitutes 'fun' for you and to incorporate it into your entrepreneurial journey to make it more enjoyable.

Pillar 8: Future. In order to remain in business you must prioritize planning for the business's growth and sustainability. I recommend a full week of annual strategic planning to review everything about your business. Use this time to set, or re-set, your annual, 3, 5, and 10- year goals. Once you have spent this kind of time planning, I recommend setting aside one day per month to review progress. Make adjustments based on new information, new networks formed, and shifts in the industry or marketplace within which you do business.

Prioritizing the future also entails working on the legacy you want to leave. Beyond the day-to-day tasks associated with planning, running, and growing a business, what do you want people to remember about you? This includes asking yourself, "What difference will your life make at the end of the journey?" I believe that my significance is that I give voice to people's dreams and potential by inspiring, educating, motivating, coaching, and engaging them in life-changing discussions and activities.

WHAT KEEPS YOU UP AT NIGHT?

When taking on a new executive coaching client, one of the first things I seek to explore is "what keeps them up at night?" The heart of this question is to figure out how their priorities are being compromised in their day-to-day activities. In exploring this further, I ask them to take me through a day in the life of how they spend their time. I then devise a "status-role" framework that reflects all the main statuses they occupy, as well as the roles and responsibilities associated with each. Then we discuss issues of ambiguity, conflict, and strain. When we get to the heart of the issue that is keeping them up at night, it is typically some valued priority being compromised. As an executive coach, I recommend spending some time revisiting key aspects of your social structure and how you function in the world as an authentic entrepreneur.

Status. First examine your status set. A status set is all the ascribed and acquired positions you occupy. For example, wife, mother, worker, sorority sister are all acquired statuses, meaning you took actions to become this particular status. However, ascribed statuses are those that are bestowed upon you through no actions of your own, such as sister, daughter, or combinations such as "Black woman". Then there is the notion of a "master status," which is the primary status by which others most identify you as. The issue is the potential for conflict between what YOU believe is your master status in comparison to what OTHERS believe is your master status.

Clearly when there is a disconnect between your self-identified master status and the one others call your master status, there is room for priorities to be compromised as you seek to re-define your master status or live up to someone's assumption of your master status. For example, at certain growth phases, you are "all boss" and all other statuses might take a backseat. As you press ahead on achieving a particular business goal you need to communicate to the people you characterize as priorities in your life that for a period of time your master status has shifted and you may be less available as you pursue a particular objective. Give them an estimated date when they might expect you to shift master statuses back to one they had grown accustomed to depending on.

Role. Every status has a set of roles and responsibilities defined as the specific behaviors expected of an individual who occupies a given status. Also, each role has an expected script. By design, taking on the role of entrepreneur changes all previously issued scripts. It is your responsibility to provide new language and change the communications about what is expected of you within the overall status-role set as the role of entrepreneur gains momentum. When pillars of priority are out of sync you want to have a candid conversation about what is expected of you in the various roles.

Role Ambiguity. Because roles largely are predicated upon the expectations of others, it is not uncommon for individuals to experience times when they are not clear on the tasks, activities, and interactions associated with each various role. Becoming a new wife and mother is where a lot of women experience role ambiguity, as they are not really sure in the early months and even years what the roles and responsibilities attached to these new statuses require of them. Becoming a new entrepreneur can also bring on role ambiguity because you know how to be an employee, but learning the role of an entrepreneur is new and different. While a difficult undertaking, you have to gain role clarity, which may mean re-scripting some roles altogether.

Role Conflict. Role conflict is when the responsibilities attached to different statuses clash. For example, as a mother, you are expected to provide primary care for minor children, in particular. As an entrepreneur you are expected to mentor and manage new employees, if you have some.

In some instances, both your minor child and new employee may need you at the same time on a Saturday morning to support their endeavours. You must resolve the conflict. This is where your pre-determined priorities come into play. As you take on greater responsibility as an entrepreneur, you will experience role conflict and will often find yourself being pulled in various directions as you attempt to respond to the many statuses you hold.

If you are a woman entrepreneur who also is a mother and, or wife, it is highly likely that you will experience role conflict over "second shift" duties. Second shift duties are comprised of those domestic chores that must still be done after working a job outside the home. Our society is socially constructed to expect that women will bear a greater load of the housework, cooking, and child-rearing. If this is the case for you, you will need to review your priorities and be real clear on what you value about each role. If you have a supportive partner or co-parent, consider renegotiating the second shift duties to be more practical and appropriate for your family unit and your entrepreneurial goals.

Role strain. Role strain is defined as having difficulties living up to all the expectations within a particular status. Many entrepreneurs will also experience role strain. For example as an entrepreneur you are responsible for growing your business, which puts you in the role of new business developer. You are also responsible for maintaining any current business you have won, which requires you to be a manager. This will no doubt stretch you, the entrepreneur, to both extremes of growth and maintenance. The key is to communicate to your team that you wear many hats in your role as an entrepreneur. Highlight that sometimes you will be quite the charismatic and charming entrepreneur as you build relationships and new business, and at other times you will be a micro-manager monitoring progress and overseeing details.

The bottom line is you have to take full responsibility for communicating and guiding people who matter through the changes being made to the scripts and norms that they had become accustomed to seeing and hearing. The best way to accomplish this is to revisit and re-assess your core values as they relate to your beliefs about what is good, right, and proper according to your priorities. Once you have reassessed your values, use them to realign your status-role set to be more practical for entrepreneurial pursuits.

CONNECTING YOUR LIFE PURPOSE TO YOUR EVERYDAY PRIORITIES

The five (5) questions below provide a simple framework for revisiting your core values and connecting the theory of what you want to accomplish with your daily practices to assure you are making progress without compromising your purpose or your clearly defined priorities.

1. **LIFE PURPOSE:** What am I called to do as an entrepreneur?
2. **CORE VALUES:** What do I value most?
3. **RESULTS:** What are the end goals tied to my pursuit of entrepreneurship?
4. **PLAN:** What strategies should I undertake to accomplish each goal?
5. **PRIORITIES:** How do I order my everyday tasks to be sure I am making progress on achieving my overall purpose?

MY "DRIVING" LESSONS LEARNED
IN PRIORITIZING

1. **MASTER LIFE.** I used the core themes from the "Master Life" devotional study in my entrepreneurial pursuit as a constant reminder that every "master plan" must pass the test of the "Master's Plan".

2. **MENTAL WELLNESS.** I set a personal wellness plan in action and learned to honor my mental health days. I take special care to rejuvenate after experiencing a personal tragedy or traumatic event even if it means passing on some business opportunities. I make time for guilty pleasures such as spa days, listening to live bands, spoken word, make-overs and photo shoots.

3. **MASTER STATUS: MOTIVATOR.** Your master status is the most important status to you and the roles attached to that status. I asked myself the question "What on earth am I here for?" I am here to motivate!

4. **MOMAGER.** Give staff permission and space to deal with life's crises, but don't allow them to wallow. Don't try to solve employees' and sub-contractors' personal problems.

5. **MILESTONES.** Celebrate professional and personal milestones with staff.

6. **MANAGEMENT.** I assign timelines and deadlines to all tasks. This gives me greater control over my schedule, and I lock people into dates and times. I also block out times I am unavailable.

7. **MAJORS AND MINORS.** I frame every so called disaster with these words "in five years, will this even matter?" My major issues are related to my core values. Minor issues are those things that will not matter in a few years.

8. **MONITORING.** I learned to detect when team members were trying to hide mistakes, missteps, and mishaps. I expose cover-ups very early and confront the issue, not the person. In redirecting or correcting, I am firm on principles and flexible on processes and practices.

9. **MISSION.** I revisit my mission statement on an annual basis prior to setting the agenda for business objectives for an upcoming year. I also review the work from the previous year to be sure we are not approaching "mission creep".

10. **MIRACLES.** I continue to believe in miracles.

"When your priorities are in conflict with your practices, have the courage to make the necessary adjustments to re-center based on your core values."

Dr. Quinn Motivates

Now Let's Go!

CHAPTER 10
ARE YOU PREPARED TO PUNCH A CLOCK THAT NEVER STOPS?
Before giving up your 9-5" be very clear that you can execute "24-7!"'

"Entrepreneurship is a lifestyle."
Dr. Quinn Motivates

There comes a moment in the life of every entrepreneur where you are faced with destiny and doom. The decision to choose destiny over doom comes down to one fundamental question: "How Bad do You Want It?" Do you want it bad enough to begin again for as many times as it takes to get the business up and running? Do you want it bad enough to accept that every buck is made because of you; and every buck stops with you; that you are 100 percent responsible for the success or failure of everything about the business venture? Are you ready to embrace and embody the life of an authentic entrepreneur where you symbolically sign up to punch a clock that never stops?

One of the biggest misconceptions of authentic entrepreneurs is that we set our own hours and plan our own schedules. Nothing could be further from the truth. Not only are you required to be responsive to the needs and deliverables of existing customers, but you must also invest an inordinate amount of time in building new business. To further complicate your schedule, you must manage staff and partners hired to work with or for your organization. In fact, as you come to understand and embrace fully all that comes with the entrepreneurial way of life as your new normal, you will discover that in essence you have signed up to punch a clock that never stops. I don't mean that you are running non-stop without appropriate breaks, rest, relaxation, and recalibration, but I do mean you have to be flexible, opportunistic, and disciplined enough to work odd hours to grow your business.

The primary reason why you must be able and willing to go "24-7" is because as the CEO you are responsible for growing and maintaining your business. This means that every day you make decisions about the future of the entrepreneurial endeavor, as well as monitor at some level the execution of current business. The reality is authentic entrepreneurship is a lifestyle not to be entered into lightly. Not only must you be competent in your chosen area of pursuit, but you must embrace all the business and operations duties that come with entrepreneurship. As I conclude this book I want to leave you with this final acronym to remind you of what it means to be committed to the "entrepreneurial way of life" as your new normal.

E: Emotional Intelligence

E	N	T	R	E	P	R	E	N	E	U	R

"The entrepreneur must grasp the concept of emotional intelligence as head work, heart work, hard work, and heroic work. But make no mistakes that intelligence nets nothing until it is activated as work."

Dr. Quinn Motivates

As an entrepreneur, you will need to make decisions using your "emotional intelligence. In its simplest definition, emotional intelligence is the ability to bridge the gap between what is happening in your head and what you are feeling in your heart. A first step in establishing emotional intelligence is to be fully aware of "self." Self-awareness during the decision-making process is crucial as you need to be fully conscious of your emotions, strengths, weaknesses, motives, values, and goals as guiding principles for your decision-making. Additionally, you want to consider the impact of your business decisions on others in your personal and professional spheres of influence. To learn more about emotional intelligence and its application for entrepreneurship, I recommend reading books written by Dr. Daniel Goleman, a psychologist who researches and consults leaders on how to create healthy work environments using core elements of emotional intelligence.

N: Networking

E N T R E P R E N E U R

"Networking is a deliberate process for moving from contact, to conversation, to making a connection, to obtaining a contract for services or cash for a product."
Dr. Quinn Motivates

One of the biggest mistakes many new entrepreneurs make is becoming engrossed in "working in" their business and they forget the necessity to "work on" generating new business. A great way to ensure you constantly are working on your business is to be engaged fully in the process of networking. Networking is not just being seen and collecting contact information at various events. It is more about being at the right events for your brand, and ultimately is about "turning contacts into contracts or cash." Not only are you networking but you must instill in your team that everyone is responsible indirectly for new business development, and if possible make it part of their performance objectives. Don't be afraid to network in non-traditional circles. The art and science of networking is different for every industry, however here are some general principles that work no matter the industry.

Write a subject matter expert book. Consider self-publishing a book that documents your perspectives on a subject matter where you have distinct expertise. Use the book as a networking tool by offering to do "free book talks" among groups of interested people. If you are in the consulting business, self-publishing is a great way to build your network and brand, and make some passive income as a book can sell even when you are not even actively marketing it. In addition, some who are considering utilizing your services may purchase your book as a first step to vet your philosophy and approach to consulting in your area of expertise. A Google search on "self-publishing" will result in thousands of resources and options for pursuing authorship. I suggest you invest some time in outlining the pros and cons of the various strategies for self-publishing within the context of your overall brand strategy and business goals.

Host or attend a monthly or quarterly event. Creating a new or integrating into an existing small group network is key. I am a proponent of non-traditional events as lunches, receptions, and dinners have become quite stale in my opinion. I prefer events that promote room movement and increase chances of meeting and interacting with individuals you normally would not have without the aid of a facilitated discussion or activity. If you host an event, create a value-proposition where people will pay for their own meal and materials to be part of the environment. Consider non-traditional things like "entrepreneur's sip and paint night," a day-party with a purpose, karaoke and creativity night, just to name few options for integrating fun into the networking occasion.

Send out an e-mail blast. Although most people are supporters of social media blasts, I prefer e-mail updates that go directly to an email address an individual has provided me. The problem with social media is that you don't control if people will see your information as it is part of a newsfeed of diverse types of posts that may grab someone's attention or not. Email blasts work best when the list-serv (a group list of recipients) is comprised of individuals you have actually met in various networking settings. Use e-mail blasts to highlight new products and services, provide updates on company achievements, profile clients and customers using your brand to solve a problem, provide industry resources and information, invite people to events, or to direct them to your point of purchase.

Turn contacts into contracts. No matter which networking strategy you select, the bottom line is you must follow-up and ask for the business, which equates to closing the deal. Once you leave a networking event, spend time "reflecting and vetting." Reflect upon who was in the room, the conversations you had, and ways in which your brand or business can be elevated by following up with key people you met. Prior to following up, however, I suggest you vet these individuals via a Google search of their website, or social media sites. You may also determine if you know people who can vouch for an individual as a credible business person. Finally, sort your follow-ups into key categories comprised of those to plug into your general contact list, those with whom you will touch base, and those who should be contacted within 72 hours on the basis of some business objective discussed during the networking event. When presenting the details of a business opportunity, always have a win-win proposition. Within the proper context, move forward with asking individuals to consider purchasing your product or services. For example, if you have a consulting business, ask for a contract. If you have a product for sale, ask for a purchase order.

T: TRANSFORMATIVE LEADERSHIP

| E | N | **T** | R | E | P | R | E | N | E | U | R |

"If you have not led a team through a crisis complete with internal threats to your integrity and systems and external forces aiming missiles at all your competitive advantages and resources then you have not mastered the art of execution."

Dr. Quinn Motivates

As an authentic entrepreneur it is your responsibility to know when, why and under what conditions you will be transforming your business. As you transform, you will need to become savvy in flowing seamlessly between extreme aspects of leadership and management. In my own work on bridging the gap between leadership and management, I have identified four (4) distinct styles that all entrepreneurs must master and be ready to adapt as they transition the business through key phases, including start-up, growth, sustainability, and exit. I provide a brief summary of the four (4) leadership and management styles below. For a more in-depth understanding of these leadership and management styles I recommend you read another one of my books titled *"Leadership Matters: Bridging the Gap between Transformational and Transactional Principles for Maximum Organizational Effectiveness."*

1. *The crisis/change leader.* The crisis or change leader's persona is effective when you face organizational crisis or reorganization, roll out a new product or service, or must defend your brand fiercely against competition. In this capacity, you are results-driven and must remain focused on the goal. It is important to note that this level of transformational leadership is very dominant and aggressive, and needs to be tempered with some softer skills.

2. *The charismatic leader.* You want to present yourself as a charismatic leader when you are pitching for new business. Internally, you want to begin a new roll-out by rallying employees and key partners around a common goal with a united front and purpose. Even in the middle of crisis and change, you want to infuse charismatic moments to keep morale high and to highlight the people who are doing a great job in pressing towards the goal. You also want to implement creative ways to communicate progress and recalibration if the in initial strategy needs to be altered.

3. *The completion manager.* If you want to increase your opportunities to hire excellent managers, you need to put yourself in the management seat. This is where you focus on institutionalizing all the technical, operations, and administrative protocols for effectiveness and efficiency in running the day-to-day business functions. In this capacity, you want to document every task that must be duplicated with precision. This is the only way to hold a manager accountable for maintaining the quality and performance of existing business while you continue to pursue new business opportunities.

4. *The thought leader.* As the thought leader, you are responsible for being the "Chief Innovative Officer". You don't have to generate every new idea, but you are responsible for creating an environment that advances the best thinking among your team. In addition, as a thought leader, you must be able to think on multiple levels. For example, to implement promising new thoughts, you have to be quick on your feet to determine its implications on people, processes, and profits. Also as a thought leader, never lose sight of your need to think about core

values and how to operationalize them in the day-to-day business environment. Finally, the thought leader things about her people and how to keep them fully engaged.

R: RHYTHM, ROUTINES, AND RITUALS

| E | N | T | **R** | E | P | R | E | N | E | U | R |

"Entrepreneurs march to the beat of their own drum."
Dr. Quinn Motivates

The entrepreneur's rhythm. Determining your most productive rhythm is paramount. For entrepreneurs, you will want to do your innovative and creative work during times you tend to have the most energy. My most productive times are at the top of the morning uninterrupted, then very late at night. In between time I do more administrative, technical, management, meetings, and problem-solving activities. Finally, no matter how hard or hectic the days, I take a mid-day break to re-focus and re-center my energy. Sometimes this results in a power nap, music break, or wellness activity.

The entrepreneur's personal routine. The great paradox in being your own boss is setting your own hours. To the extent possible, incorporate personal activities that matter into your entrepreneurial schedule. For example, Sundays and Wednesday nights are marked on my schedule as "church." In addition, I begin each day with prayer and meditation, followed by a short writing session. Also on Sunday afternoons, I spend two (2) hours prepping for meetings, reviewing the schedule for the week, touching base with people on the schedule, and finalizing technical notes to staff. I also plan my wardrobe, meal occasions, personal grooming needs, and work-out time according to my meetings and consulting schedule for the week. Finally when I worked a full weekend, I take Mondays off to rejuvenate.

The entrepreneur's business routines. In addition to personal routines, you need to institutionalize some business routines. For example, I refer to Mondays as "Administrative Mondays" where I am in full business and operations mode in terms of paying bills, reviewing invoices, sending out e-mails, reviewing and submitting reports, and checking in with staff individually, and in meetings. If at all possible I try to avoid client meetings on Mondays. I call Tuesday "Technical Tuesdays" where I focus in on the projects that require my technical leadership and expertise. On "Wellness Wednesdays" I take four (4) hours of down time to think, rejuvenate, and recalibrate. Thursdays are my troubleshooting days where I go hard on problem-solving and strategic thinking. Fridays are known as "Follow- up Fridays" where I return phone calls, respond to e-mails, and address anything else that slipped through the cracks all week.

The team's rhythm. As you begin to bring on more permanent sub-contractors and employees in particular, you will need to integrate the various "rhythms" to maximize teamwork. This is an important undertaking in helping a team synergize diverse talents and skills. As a firm grows, team rhythm becomes institutionalized as the corporate culture. Therefore, it is imperative that you set standards and only sanction team rhythm activities that promote your firm's core values. At the same time, be open to allowing some rhythmic activities to be "membership-grown." For example, living in the metro-Atlanta area, and working with many single mothers, I learned to hold important team meetings between the hours of 10:00 AM and 2:00 PM to allow people to manage their diverse priorities and navigate the unpredictable traffic problems. Second, I encourage the team to decorate their workstations with personal photos and other things that bring them comfort, and I allow them to play their music, and use their social media sites during normal work hours. I have mandatory seasonal office shut downs to symbolize the need to refresh and rejuvenate. Also, if the workload is under control, I try to end the work day by 3:00 PM on Fridays. I have had to be careful with this one as some people take advantage and actually plan on being off by that time as a right, and not a privilege; while others pushed the Friday leave from 3:00 PM to noon. I have tried various configurations of work-from-home and am only able to report "mixed results" in this regard after ten (10) years in the business. However, the point is to work with your team to determine the rhythmic flow based on what motivates, empowers, and energizes them to do their best work and have enthusiasm for other aspects of their lives as well.

The team's routines. Team routines are more formal and should be part of your standard operating procedures. For team routines, focus on those tasks that could result in legal, IRS, fiscal, or contractual issues due to non-compliance. You must establish that these routine administrative activities are to be done by all staff no matter their title or position. Examples include reporting time and attendance on time and within protocol, accounting for business expenses, and using proper channels for complaints and grievances. It is not just enough issue operating manuals, you must engage, discuss, and reiterate even routine and mundane tasks. It may sound like overkill, but as new people enter, you don't want them to read one set of rules, and observe staff cutting corners and breaking rules, and not meeting the consequences outlined in the protocol. You also want to send a message that you are never too busy building new business that you lose all touch with the day-to-day operations.

The team's rituals. In addition to rhythms and routines, teams need rituals defined as the times set aside to celebrate or mark milestones along the path of entrepreneurship. Some of these include "The Annual President's Summit" where every January I take the time to prepare my team for the journey of the coming year by reflecting on lessons learned from the previous year, skills-building for some new area of focus for the coming year, and setting the strategic plan of action in motion. Every August we celebrate the company's anniversary. Other rituals that work for my firm include: (1) all available staff joining new employees for lunch during the first week of employment; and (2) the good job shout outs via e-mail when an employee or contracting partner has gone above the call of duty to problem-solve or take a project to a pristine finish.

E: Ethics

E N T R E P R E N E U R

"I am not going to jail or hell for breaking the laws governing business ownership."
Dr. Quinn Motivates

No matter how fast-paced your pursuit to build your business, never ever compromise ethics. That is, don't cut corners, don't cheat, and don't break the law to get your business up and running. Don't hide any income from the IRS. In addition, hold everyone that works for you accountable for the resources entrusted to them to get their jobs done. No matter your adherence to ethical principles, disgruntled employees or partners seeking revenge may attack you or accuse you of unethical practices. I have listed below a number of things to consider in setting up your business and operations to address ethics.

1. Follow all IRS rules and regulations governing small-business ownership.
2. Meet all your contractual obligations or communicate and renegotiate deadlines and scopes of work if possible.
3. Maintain detailed accounting controls and financial record-keeping.
4. Keep comprehensive human resources and teaming agreement records of performance and reprimands according to policy or contractual clauses.
5. On-board employees and sub-contractors with written policies and guidelines in a way that sends a strong message that no one is exempt from meeting ethical expectations.
6. Integrate discussions on ethics into the everyday work environment.
7. Invest in courageous followers who set a moral example for peers and subordinates.

P: Project Management

> *"Resist the need to cut corners and take short cuts. Traditional business principles and practices get the job done every time."*
>
> *Dr. Quinn Motivates*

As your entrepreneurial enterprise becomes more complex with multiple products, services, and clients, you will need to establish a strong project management system to be sure that staff and sub-contractors understand the overall perspective on "high standards," "high quality," "stellar performance", and "effective productivity". The main thing I had to do for my team was to separate "activity" from "productivity" and distinguish between professional polish and finished products as opposed to what employees had been deemed "good enough" in previous work and educational settings. You will need to become a quick study of core concepts used in project management as listed below:

1. *Scope and scope change management.* Scope is the way you define the boundaries of the project. It determines what the project will deliver and what it will not deliver.

2. *Project manager.* The person with the most authority and oversight associated with the day-to-day operations of a product or service's implementation or market penetration plan.

3. *Deliverables.* All projects create deliverables. A deliverable is any tangible outcome that is expected to be produced by the project.

4. *Work plan.* The project work plan tells you how you will complete the project. It describes the activities required, the sequence of the work, who is assigned to the work, an estimate of how much effort is required, when the work is due, and other information of interest to the project manager.

5. *Critical path.* The critical path is the sequence of activities that must be completed on schedule and in what order for the entire project to be completed on schedule.

6. *Milestone.* A milestone is an event that signifies the completion of a major deliverable or a set of related deliverables.

R: RELATIONSHIPS

| E | N | T | R | E | P | **R** | E | N | E | U | R |

"Effective relationships are essential to building and sustaining a business."

Dr. Quinn Motivates

The relationship dilemma for entrepreneurs is complex because you must become a good judge of character and you will have to make "gut" decisions about people as partners and employees. My perspective on relationships is to be vulnerable and transparent enough to own all that comes with the territory of entrepreneurship. As an entrepreneur committed to growing your business, you will outgrow some people personally and professionally. This doesn't mean that you don't still care about them or that you don't want a relationship with them. It simply means that the relationship must be redefined to fit the reality of where you are going within the context of others' lack of interest, will, or capacity to go with you to the next level. On a personal level, should you experience tension or turmoil, recognize the importance of healthy relationships with close family and friends, and resolve to restore broken relationships that are truly important to you.

E: EQUITY

| E | N | T | R | E | P | R | **E** | N | E | U | R |

"Never underestimate the value of sweat equity, which is the combination of hard work and hustle."

Dr. Quinn Motivates

As an entrepreneur you will need to think about equity on two levels. First, in the early years of your business, you primarily will be more consumed with sweat equity. Sweat equity is about rolling up your sleeves and doing the dirty, mundane work to keep costs low while you build a robust business and operations system. Building sweat equity is the grit and grind that ultimately becomes "ownership interest", as it increases the value of a brand or enterprise over time. At some point, sweat equity will be measured in traditional indicators of financial equity where your financial statements will reflect your efforts to maximize profit and shareholders' wealth, while minimizing cost and business losses.

N: NURTURING

"Nurturing your inner circle means weaning them off milk, teaching them to chew meat, then ultimately showing them how to hunt for their own food."

Dr. Quinn Motivates

Nurturing others as an entrepreneur centers on caring about your people's personal and professional growth. You have to strike a fine balance of being empathetic and enterprising. Nurturing also entails having the courage to engage staff and partners in difficult conversations to reconcile disconnects between daily routines and aspirations for excellence. In order to recognize your options, limits, and opportunities to nurture others in the workplace, you must determine the extent to which your preferred nurturing style is appropriate for diverse groups of people. For example, some only respond to softer caregiving and are paralyzed by tough love approaches. Others do extremely well when coached to take risks or perform at another level of excellence, while a few will literally quit rather than be coached out of their comfort zone.

E: Exit Strategy

| E | N | T | R | E | P | R | E | N | **E** | U | R |

"Knowing your end game will shape key decisions in your business strategy."
Dr. Quinn Motivates

For the passionate entrepreneur who found a way to turn a hobby into a money-making lifestyle, asking you to create an exit strategy at first glance may appear counterintuitive as it relates to why you set up the business in the first place. However, a better way to think about exit strategy is to envision the legacy you want to leave; then begin with the end in mind. In chapter five (5) on setting up robust business management and operating systems, I discussed having an exit strategy. I recommend you review those notes annually to determine if there are any shifts that may require a redirect in your initial thinking and planning on appropriate exit strategies.

U: Unapologetically Ambitious

| E | N | T | R | E | P | R | E | N | E | **U** | R |

"Be unapologetically ambitious!"
Dr. Quinn Motivates

Over the years I have studied the backstories of thousands of entrepreneurs. While they have many things in common, the one that stands out the most is the turning point in their pursuit where they became unapologetic about the time, the grind, the commitment, and ultimately the success. I am fascinated by how many of them manage to live a stress-free and guilt-free life. What I came to discover is they can live with this unprecedented degree of freedom because they resist criticism, negativity, jealousy, envy, and hate that would consume their time in trying to respond. I have coined the phrase *"unapologetically ambitious"* to describe the way they tend to respond to the combined forces of negativity by simply continuing to do what they love and repeating the cycle of success. In essence, rather than spend energy and time explaining and justifying their actions to people who don't matter, they unapologetically pour all of their energy into the next great thing on their vision board. The *"unapologetically ambitious"* ignore the bullies and the public discourse of people hurling unfounded judgmental comments their way, and throwing unsubstantiated catch phrases such as, she is crazy, cut throat, unethical, lacking character, insensitive, unreasonable, and out of control. The *"unapologetically ambitious"* even find a way to forego the need to respond to bystanders who listen attentively as others find faults and flaws in their pursuits. Instead, the *"unapologetically ambitious"* get busy building up their brand, their business, and giving the naysayers more to talk about.

R: RELENTLESS

E	N	T	R	E	P	R	E	N	E	U	R

"Authentic entrepreneurs possess a relentless drive to find a way or figure it out; but under no circumstances do they fold under pressure."
Dr. Quinn Motivates

You have to be relentless in your pursuit of entrepreneurship. Resolve that you are a long distance driver, who will put the petal to the metal and go! There will be times when you will not feel as driven as the day before. Drive on anyway. As a matter of face, you will wake up some mornings and find your desire to drive greatly diminished. You have my permission to put it in park on those days.

Being relentless means learning from your failures and vowing to remain "all in" in order to maximize your opportunities for running and growing your business. When your business reaches a turning point, then turn up your commitment to give it all you got. Hold each team member accountable in ways that signify that you genuinely care about their success even if they are not willing or unable to go the distance.

When faced with family crises, and friends who don't understand the thrill of the entrepreneur hustle, keep driving. Drive in the morning at the crack of dawn. Drive through your lunch break. Drive during dinner. Drive yourself to bed, and as you drift off to sleep thinking about driving the next day. Simply refuse to be driven off the road by road ragers called obstacles, odds, barriers or barricades. Instead, look for new ways to drive more efficiently, more effectively, and ultimately, drive towards increased profitability.

Being relentless means pursuing your entrepreneurial goal even when others don't get it. Pull over and let them get out of the car or put them out, but you have to DRIVE on. You may have been headed in the same direction for a long stretch of road, but when it becomes abundantly clear, that you are on separate journeys, lighten your load. Some will call you names, take cheap shots, kick the very car they are riding in, put sugar in your fuel tank, slash your tires, or even give you the wrong driving directions as evil efforts to slow you down or throw you off course. You can stop for a tune-up and repair the damage they have done. But never stop driving.

Refuse to give a place to haters. Don't heckle them. Don't post about them. Don't entertain them. Instead, drown them out by turning up the volume of your entrepreneurial pursuit and drive to your customized soundtrack called "success." Turn up more excellence. Turn up high performance. Turn up team-work. Turn up the tenacity. And when you finally do turn down for rest, don't be weary even when you are exhausted because it is better to be exhausted from giving it all you got than to be well-rested from having achieved nothing.

Accept that the entrepreneurial life cycle includes some difficult decisions and times with staff and partners. You must make tough decisions anyway. Not all investors will understand or agree with recalibrated strategies and tactics, but you must recalibrate anyway. You will discover that not every business partner and teaming agreement has your best business interest at heart. Be open to doing partnerships and teaming agreements anyway!

And as you move your business up and out into unchartered waters, NOT everyone will be willing to follow you courageously. You must move forward anyway. No matter what, somehow, someway vow to keep driving when others give in, give up, or give out! You keep driving with an entrepreneurial spirit to give it all you got!

MY "DRIVING" LESSONS LEARNED
IN LIVING THE AUTHENTIC ENTREPRENEURIAL LIFE

1. **ANOINTED.** I came to understand that my entrepreneurial spirit is reflective of all the gifts and talents God gave me.

2. **AMBITIONS.** I made peace with my overly ambitious self and shifted my circle to be surrounded by others who are just as hungry as I am. We hunt together. We eat together. We celebrate together.

3. **AUTHENTIC.** I realize that my brand authenticity is grounded in the multi-dimensional, multi-talented ways in which I acquire and apply diverse knowledge and experiences for profit.

4. **ALL IN.** In August of 2012, was the first time I resolved to be "all-in." Although I started my business in 2005, I kept part-time teaching jobs at leading research universities. From 2009 to 2011, I completed a post-doctoral fellowship. What I came to realize is that while the income was decent, more importantly I was using university-based opportunities as security blankets and comfort zones.

5. **ATTITUDE.** When I learned not to take anything personal or for granted, my disposition and demeanor became a lot more polished.

6. **AFFIRMATIONS.** I came to view affirmation as a way to speak positively to pain.

7. **ACHIEVEMENT-ORIENTED.** I developed an "ACHIEVE" model to serve as a constant reminder of the results sought in: "Affirm your Aspirations", "Confirm your Commitment", "Harmonize your Head, Heart, Hands, and Habits", "Ignite Innovative Ideas", "Eliminate Excuses", Visualize Victory, and "Execute with Excellence".

8. **ACTION-ORIENTED.** Entrepreneurs don't have problems. We have decisions to make. To the extent possible re-invest profits to finance your company's growth and to have operating capital on hand for cash flow issues. Don't celebrate and liquidate too early.

9. **ANALYTICAL.** I learned how to analyze using a concept I call "think and move" where I blend the art and science of being creative with sound business decision-making to advance my entrepreneurial goals.

10. **AMAZING.** I finally accepted that I am the proverbial poster child of amazing grace!

"When it comes to entrepreneurship, just before you give up, give out, or give in, I challenge you to give it all you got!"

Dr. Quinn Motivates

Now Let's Go!

RECOMMENDATIONS FOR 100 BOOKS TO HELP KEEP YOUR "DRIVING" SKILLS SHARP!

I am a proponent of continuing education and have come to appreciate formal classroom instruction, as well as self-directed studies. Over the years, I have found pleasure in planning my own studies in a number of subject matter areas. Yes, I can come across as a walking encyclopedia of sorts. However, in conversation with authentic entrepreneurs, I am constantly asked to recommend books for them to read on business development and professional growth in general. To help keep your "DRIVING" skills sharp, I have provided a list of 100 books organized by the chapter topics in my book. I have included recently published books, as well as some classics that I believe represent timeless advice and strategies for moving your business to the next level.

CHAPTER 1: ARE YOU READY TO SHIFT FROM A CAREER TO A CALLING?

1	*"In Pursuit of Purpose: Biblical Guidance for the Entrepreneurial Journey"* by Dr. Quinn (2016)
2	*"Act Like a Success, Think Like a Success: Discovering Your Gift and the Way to Life's Riches"* by Steve Harvey (2014)
3	*"DARE: Straight Talk on Confidence, Courage, and Career for Women in Charge"* by Becky Blalock (2013)
4	*"Help Yourself: How to Create a Whole New You, More Income, and a Better Life"* by Becky A. Davis (2013)
5	*"Start Where You Are: Life Lessons in Getting from Where You are to Where You Want to Be"* by Chris Gardner (2010)
6	*"Be All You Can Be: A Challenge to Stretch to Your God-Given Potential"* by John C. Maxwell (2007)
7	*"The Road Less Traveled: A New Psychology of Love, Traditional Values, and Spiritual Growth"* by M. Scott Peck (2003)
8	*"The Purpose-Driven Life: What On Earth Am I Here For?"* by Rick Warren (2002)
9	*"The Seat of the Soul"* by Gary Zukav (1989)
10	*"As a Man Thinketh"* by James Allen (1903)

Chapter 2: Do you have a Healthy Flow of Authentic Enthusiasm?

1. "The Holy Bible"
2. "It's Time for the Motivator: 40 Achievement Principles for Maximizing Your Full Potential" by Dr. Quinn (2016)
3. "Order My Steps: Learning to Walk the Path that's Ordered by God" by Sheretta West (2014)
4. "Think and Grow Rich" by Napoleon Hill (2010)
5. "The Prayer of Jabez: Breaking Through to the Blessed Life" by Bruce Wilkinson (2000)
6. "A is for Attitude: An Alphabet for Living" by Patricia Russell-McCloud (1999)
7. "Transform Your Life" by Barbara King (1995)
8. "Daily Motivations for African-American Success" by Dennis Kimbro (1993)
9. "Six Attitudes for Winners" by Norman Vincent Peale (1989)
10. "The Positive Principle Today" by Norman Vincent Peale (1976)

Chapter 3: Are you Willing to Re-Purpose your Past?

1. "Living Positively One Day at a Time" by Robert Schuller (1980)
2. "Good Self, Bad Self: How to Bounce Back from a Personal Crisis" by Judy Smith (2013)
3. "The Fruit of the Spirit: Becoming the Person God Wants You to Be" by Thomas E. Trask and Wayd I. Goodall (2010)
4. "One Day My Soul Just Opened Up: 40 Days and 40 Nights toward Spiritual Strength and Personal Growth" by Iyanla Vanzant (1998)
5. "Sacred Pampering Principles: An African American Woman's Guide to Self-care and Inner Renewal" by Debrena Jackson Gandy (1997)
6. "Lessons in Living" by Susan L. Taylor (1995)
7. "The Value in the Valley: A Black Women's Guide Through Life's Dilemmas" by Iyanla Vanzant (1996)
8. "Peace from Broken Pieces: How to Get Through What You're Going Through" by Iyanla Vanzant (2012)
9. "The Four Agreements: A Practical Guide to Personal Freedom" by Dan Miguel Ruiz (1997)
10. "Pace Yourself: Daily Devotions for Those Who do Too Much" by Ric Engram (1992)

Chapter 4: Do You Have a Clearly Defined Brand?

1. *"The Power of Visual Storytelling: How to Use Visuals, Videos, and Social Media to Market Your Brand"* by Ekaterina Walter and Jessica Gioglio (2015)
2. *"What Great Brands Do: The Seven Brand-Building Principles That Separate the Best From the Rest"* by Denise Lee Yohn (2014)
3. *"Look the Part to Get the Role"* by Brandi Mitchell (2013)
4. *"Profit with Purpose: A Marketer's Guide to Delivering Purpose-driven Campaigns to Multi-cultural Audiences"* by Teneshia Jackson Warner (2012)
5. *"Duct Tape Marketing"* by John Jantsch (2011)
6. *"Guerilla Marketing: Easy and Inexpensive Strategies for Making Big Profits from Your Small Business"* by Jay Conrad Levinson (2007)
7. *"The Art of Social Media: Subtitle: Power Tips for Power Users"* by Guy Kawasaki and Peg Fitzpatrick (2007)
8. *"Influence: The Psychology of Persuasion"* by Robert Cialdini (2006)
9. *"The Life of PT Barnum"* by P.T. Barnum (2004)
10. *"Oprah Winfrey Speaks: Insight from the World's Most Influential Voice"* by Janet Lowe (2001)

Chapter 5: Have You Mastered Business Management 101?

1. *"The Five Most Important Questions You will Ever Ask about your Organization"* by Peter F. Drucker (2008)
2. *"Manager's Toolkit: The 13 Skills Managers Need to Succeed"* by Harvard Business School Press (2004)
3. *"The Girl's Guide to starting your own business"* by Caitlin Friedman and Kimberly Yorio (2003)
4. *"The One Minute Manager"* by Kenneth Blanchard and Spencer Johnson (2003)
5. *"What is Management: How it works and Why it's Everyone's Business"* by Joan Margretta in collaboration with Nan Stone (2002)
6. *"Managing by the Numbers: a Commonsense guide to understanding and using your company's financials"* by Chuck Kremer and Ron Rizzuto with John Case (2000)
7. *"Small Business for Dummies"* by Eric Tyson and Jim Schell (2000)
8. *"Successful Manager's Handbook: Development Suggestions for Today's Managers"* by Brian L. Davis (1996)
9. *"The Anatomy of a Business Plan"* by Linda Pinson and Jerry Jinnett (1996)
10. *"The Complete Book of Consulting"* by Bill Salmon and Nate Rosenblatt (1995)

Chapter 6: Have You Built a Vision for Your Dream Team?

1. "Dealing with People You Can't Stand: How to Bring Out the Best in People at Their Worst" by Rick Brinkman and Rick Kirschner (2012)
2. "Leading at the Edge: Leadership Lessons from the Extraordinary Saga of Shackleton's Antarctic Expedition" by Dennis N. T. Perkins (2012)
3. "Drive: The Surprising Truth Behind What Motivates Us" by Daniel Pink (2011)
4. "The Heart of a Leader: Insights on the Art of Influence" by Ken Blanchard (2007)
5. "Everybody Wins: The Chapman Guide to Solving Conflicts Without Arguing" by Gary Chapman (2006)
6. "The Servant Leader" by Blanchard and Hodges (2003)
7. "The FIVE Dysfunctions of a Team: A leadership Fable" by Patrick Lencioni (2002)
8. "Who Moved My Cheese?" By Spencer Johnson (1998)
9. "The Courageous Follower: Standing up to and for our leaders" by Ira Chaleff (1995)
10. "Bringing Out the Best in People" by Alan L. McGinnis (1985)

Chapter 7: Do You Have a Growth and Maintenance Plan?

1. "Blue Ocean Strategy, Expanded Edition: How to Create Uncontested Market Space and Make the Competition Irrelevant" by W. Chan Kim (2015)
2. "Scaling Up" by Verne Harnish (2014)
3. "Playing to Win" by A.G. Lafley and Roger L. Martin (2013)
4. "The First 90 Days, Updated and Expanded: Proven Strategies for Getting Up to Speed Faster and Smarter" by Michael Watkins (2013)
5. "War Fighting: The U.S. Marine Corps Book of Strategy" by The United States Marine Corps (2012)
6. "Onward: How Starbucks Fought for Its Life Without Losing Its Soul" by Howard Schultz (2011)
7. "Innovation and Entrepreneurship" by Peter F. Drucker (2006)
8. "The 8th Habit: From Effectiveness to Greatness" by Stephen R. Covey (2004)
9. "Good to Great: Why Some Companies Make the Leap...And Others Don't" by Jim Collins (2001)
10. "First, Break All The Rules" by Marcus Buckingham And Curt Coffman (1999)

CHAPTER 8: CAN YOU ACCEPT DEFEAT, BUT NOT FAILURE?

1. *"The Upside of Down: Why Failing Well Is the Key to Success"* by Megan McArdle (2014)
2. *"THE RISE: Creativity, the Gift of Failure, and the Search for Mastery"* by Sarah Lewis (2014)
3. *"Overcoming Your Fear of Failure: A Portion from Life After Art"* by Matt Appling (2013)
4. *"Steve Jobs"* by Walter Isaacson (2011)
5. *"Failure: The Secret to Success"* by Robby Slaughter (2011)
6. *"Failing Forward: Turning Mistakes into Stepping Stones for Success"* by John C. Maxwell (2007)
7. *"The Ugly Truth about Small Business"* by Ruth King (2005)
8. *"What Makes the Great Great"* by Dennis Kimbro (1998)
9. *"Have You Felt Like Giving Up Lately"* by David Wilkerson (1982)
10. *"All things are Possible Through Prayer"* by Charles Allen (1978)

CHAPTER 9: DO YOU HAVE A PROPER PERSPECTIVE ON YOUR PRIORITIES?

1. *"The Pursuit of HappYness* by Chris Gardner" (with Quincy Troupe) (2007)
2. *"How to Stop Worrying and Start Living: Time-tested Methods for Conquering Worry"* by Dale Carnegie (2006)
3. *"Ian K. Smith"* by Extreme Fat Smash Diet (2006)
4. *"Dr. Ro's Ten Secrets to Livin' Healthy"* by Rovenia M. Brock (2004)
5. *"The Journey from Success to Significance"* by John C. Maxwell (2004)
6. *"First Things First"* by Stephen R. Covey (1996)
7. *"The Best Kind of Loving: A Black Woman's Guide to Finding Intimacy"* by Gwendolyn Goldsby Grant (1996)
8. *"The Five Love Languages"* by Gary Chapman (1995)
9. *"Don't Sweat the Small Stuff at Work"* by Richard Carlson (1990)
10. *"The 7 Habits of Highly Effective People: Powerful Lessons in Personal Change"* by Stephen R. Covey (1989)

Chapter 10: Are You Prepared to Punch a Clock That Never Stops?

1. *"What I Know for Sure"* by Oprah Winfrey (2014)
2. *"How Remarkable Women Lead"* by Joanna Barsh and Susie Cranston (2011)
3. *"Expect to Win: 10 Proven Strategies for Thriving in the Workplace"* by Carla Harris (2010)
4. *"Starting from Scratch: Secrets from 21 Ordinary People who made the Entrepreneurial Leap"* by Wes Moss (2005)
5. *"Swim with the Sharks without being Eaten Alive"* by Harvey MacKay (2005)
6. *"How To Win Friends and Influence People"* by Dale Carnegie (1998)
7. *"Live Your Dreams"* by Les Brown (1994)
8. *"Think and Grow Rich: A Black Choice"* by Dennis Kimbro (1992)
9. *"Believe and Achieve: W. Clement Stones 17 Principles of Success"* by Samuel A. Cypert (1991)
10. *"Secrets of the World's Top Sales Performers"* by Christine Harvey (1990)

"After you've done all you can, STAND! You may be standing alone, but the good news is you are still standing! If you can stand, you can walk. If you can walk, you can run, and if you can run, you can mount up on wings and SOAR! Because I believe if you put your mind to it, you can do it…Now Let's Go!"

www.ingramcontent.com/pod-product-compliance
Lightning Source LLC
Chambersburg PA
CBHW051923160426
43198CB00012B/2020